WATERSHED

Watershed

ATTENDING TO BODY
AND EARTH IN DISTRESS

RANAE LENOR HANSON

UNIVERSITY OF MINNESOTA PRESS
Minneapolis
London

The University of Minnesota Press gratefully acknowledges the
generous assistance provided for the publication of this book by
the Margaret S. Harding Memorial Endowment, honoring the first
director of the University of Minnesota Press.

The Coda was presented by Winona LaDuke at Minneapolis Community
and Technical College during the 1990s. Material from "Life Principles of the
Ojibwe People Indigenous to Northern Minnesota Watersheds" is printed
with permission of Honor the Earth.

For maps and other resources related to *Watershed,*
please see ranaehanson.com.

Published by the University of Minnesota Press
111 Third Avenue South, Suite 290
Minneapolis, MN 55401-2520
http://www.upress.umn.edu

ISBN 978-1-5179-1097-6 (pb)

Library of Congress record available at https://lccn.loc.gov/2020058640

Printed in Canada on acid-free paper

The University of Minnesota is an equal-opportunity educator and employer.

28 27 26 25 24 23 22 21   10 9 8 7 6 5 4 3 2 1

For Minnow Lake Watershed
and all who have drunk,
and all who will drink, of its waters

The woods and waters that nourished
my youth are territories of the Ojibwe.
The college where I teach lies on Dakota
land. I offer thanks and respect to the
original people of these lands. I ask for the
blessing of the ancestors on my intentions,
on my words, and on you as you read.

CONTENTS

NAVIGATING THE WATERS
OF THIS BOOK

When you lower a canoe into a wide river, multiple points on the far shore call you toward them. A similar handful of journeys will open before you when you enter these pages.

This book follows multiple arcs, not a single straight line. Consider it a braid with varied story-strands woven together. Let yourself be taken by its currents, trusting that they will lead you to a destination that is life-giving for you. You will explore stories of group efforts to save mangrove swamps in Saudi Arabia, of drought in Ethiopia, of messages from the past on rocks above crooked rivers in northern Minnesota, of diabetic crisis in an ICU bed in St. Paul.

But the most important story you will uncover as you read will be your own. You may hear the voice of your own climate-stressed body. You may find a way home to your own watershed.

The long first chapter may cradle you and help you consider how your own bit of earth has offered you nurture. Feel welcome to compose (to write or sing or dance) your own song of thanks to the living earth that allowed you to reach this point of maturity.

Between the chapters I include shorter meditations that offer interactive suggestions. Adapt these as appropriate to your own life conditions.

If, while reading, you reach a bend or eddy or stretch of calm where your journey feels interrupted, consider paddling ashore. Jump out, portage across pages, find more nourishing waters.

As you read the messages entrusted to me by others, consider those people around you whose life trajectories and homelands may be foreign to you. As you hear how climate disruption has affected animals and plants near me, consider those close to you. You may choose to shut the book for a while and, instead, walk outside to learn from the people and other beings around you.

In this book I tell of the disease that showed up as a messenger to me. Next to my words, feel free to write the stories of your own body's challenges as well as those of others with whom you share this earth and sky.

Some threats, like COVID-19, we confront together, but paradoxically also in isolation. The community of our struggle is as real as our solitude. As you read these pages, recall and tell your stories—as an individual in a body, as a part of the human collective, as a being in an ecosystem.

In the book's Coda, you will find principles that Winona LaDuke shared at Minneapolis College. When Ms. LaDuke presented these, she explained that, through her work as a leader in the Indigenous Women's Network, she had found these ethical principles to embody most of the fundamental stances of Indigenous people across the globe. She pointed out that life principles should be passed from living tongues to living brains so that they can be molded to fit changing situations. They should not be cast in stone. With her permission, I offer her words to you, from her living culture to your living awareness.

You may want to read those principles now, allowing them to seep into your thinking, letting them wrap themselves around your own life conditions.

And then, let all the words go. It is Life that teaches us.

Your watershed may lie far from mine; it may flow differently. Yet all waters eventually flow together. They unite in mist and in clouds. All rivers join the sea.

WATERSHED

How to Live

Climate catastrophe turns up
in my body and in yours.

As the climate shifts, basic life processes
alter—spring and summer, fall and winter,
air and ocean currents, atmospheric density.
As the climate continues to change, the
new patterns, to which we may have
attempted to adapt, begin to swirl.

Lyme disease extends its reach as the landscape
warms. Diabetes, in both its forms, is increasing
on all continents at a rate faster than any
previous human disease. Climate change will
complicate the management of diabetes. Water
shortages, outdoor conditions that make
exercise difficult, pollution, novel viruses,
infrastructure instability, too much or too
little or inappropriate food—all will make
diabetes and other illnesses harder to contend
with. Some of these conditions will further
increase the number of people with disease.

Paradoxically, living in a damaged body
can teach us much about how to live
in a damaged ecosystem—and about how
to return to practices of joy.

1

WHERE WATERS DIVIDE

Spring

Each child's fate is linked to that of its natal watershed. On a late
May day, my mom finished planting her garden next to the small
trailer where she and Dad lived, just south of Lake Bemidji.

The Mississippi headwaters begin at Lake Itasca, flow north
into Lake Bemidji, then meander south toward the Gulf of Mexico. Thirty miles north of Bemidji, as far north as Itasca is south,
lies Red Lake, home waters for the Red Lake Nation of the
Ojibwe. Red Lake lets out to join the Red River, which flows north
toward Lake Winnipeg, and then to the Nelson River, and on to
Hudson Bay.

When Mom stood up to walk toward the house Dad was building, her water broke.

I came into a land fed by rain and by snow, a land of swamps
where two great river systems begin their journeys, one flowing
north and one flowing south.

Summer

Along the shores of Red Lake that summer, the ground glimmered blue with berries. Mom's and Dad's baskets overflowed.

They tented in the woods on an acre they had purchased for stumpage. The hospital stay for my birth had cost sixty-three dollars. If they could afford to finish their house, they'd have a flush toilet and could stop visiting the outhouse behind my aunt's place across the gravel road. By cutting and peeling timber, they would augment what money came from the GI Bill.

At 6:00 a.m. they'd push out of the tent, leaving me asleep inside. Dad would fell trees and Mom would peel bark. When I woke, they'd cook eggs over a fire. After breakfast, Mom would lay me on a blanket in the field, moving both it and me from one downed tree to another.

One day bees rose from the ground between her legs as she held me.

Fall

In September, Mom and Dad took me south along the path of the Mississippi to the Cities. We listened to a Bible teacher and visited the Minnesota State Fair. In the heat of the day, they cooled me with ice cream. A mile away stood the house where, four decades later, I would raise children of my own.

Winter

No major rivers flow into Minnesota. The snow and rain fall on the headwaters of four great river systems. Under the ice, the waters begin long journeys in three directions. The Mississippi flows south to the Gulf. The Red River and the White Iron Chain of Lakes each flow north to Hudson Bay. The St. Louis River joins the Great Lakes and flows northeast to the Atlantic.

The dark of winter with its blanketing snow was my early cradle and comfort. My waking, the coming of spring. I learned to stand on a land where waters divide.

Spring

My love for the beginning of spring blossomed with the smell of lilacs. I reached high above my head to grab them off branches in the alley behind the house where we lived once Dad got his first teaching job.

Our home in Wheaton lay in the Bois de Sioux Watershed, part of the Red River Basin. There spring rains brought lilacs just in time for May Day. With my mom, I wove paper baskets, filled them with candy and lilacs, and carried them to the doorsteps of other children. Mom and I would knock on the doors and then run. I'd come home to a porchful of baskets left for me. I don't remember the children. I remember the dew that dropped from the lilacs onto my hands. I remember pressing my nose into the smell.

And I remember the color of the sky when I opened my eyes after rolling down a hill. Still dizzy, I watched the world spin. Blue and green and the scent of soft earth.

Summer

One sunny day, my father's mother took me to the Mississippi headwaters at Itasca. I held her hand as we stepped from stone to stone across the beginning of what she told me would become a mighty flow. After crossing back under the pines, she and I walked together toward a man who stood in a leather shirt and leggings next to a teepee and behind a rope fence from which hung a plaque with words on it. Feeling shy, I pressed into Grandma. She said hello; he didn't answer or look toward us. I felt confused. As we walked back toward the car, Grandma said that many Indians like him had lived here "before."

My father invited a man who he said was the chief of Red Lake Reservation to dinner at our next house in Bagley. I remember a man older than my father firmly upright at the head of the table. I remember feathers. Around him, the air was still.

I expect that we held hands before eating and that Dad prayed. In that way my parents enforced community with any who ate at our house. I remember my father as earnest, then a bit jovial. Probably he spoke of Jesus to the man.

Several times during those years we fished at Red Lake. Once, we stepped from the car into a cloud of mosquitoes so thick I pinched my eyes shut. Just the same, we went out on the lake. I did not fish. I watched a walleye flopping on the wooden floor of the boat and wanted to throw him back, but I was afraid to touch his cold sides.

Fall

I grew old enough to attend the school across the road where my dad taught printing and woodwork. We pupils sat in desks placed in firm rows. In the hall, we stood single-file in lines. When I spoke once inside the bathroom, the teacher covered my picture on the classroom wall with a flap of paper and I was prevented from going to the gym for three days. We memorized the ABCs and repeated the list of letters quickly. Slow to say those letters, I was placed with the Robin Readers; our teacher liked the Bluebirds. I looked out the window; real birds flew outside.

Many Fridays, my family drove west to stay with the cousins on the farms or, Sundays early, east to visit the cousins in Bemidji.

One afternoon when we stopped to fill the tank before heading toward my grandfather's farm, I stepped near the nozzle of the hose. Dad asked me to move.

I objected. "I like to smell it."

"This smell is lead," he said. "It will poison your brain. You get back into the car."

Back in position behind him, I looked toward the trees through the window.

Minutes later I leaned forward. "Daddy," I asked in a loud voice so he could hear, "if the gas is poison, why do you put it into the air? Should we stop breathing the air?"

"The trees clean the air." His voice came back mixed with the sound of the engine. "They take the bad stuff out and put oxygen in."

Many trees slipped by as we drove. Past the other side windows, over my two brothers' heads, cars zoomed in the opposite direction. Those cars also were many. Each car fed poison to the trees. Where would the trees put it?

The farm we were going to was my uncle's, but it had been my grandpa's before that. My grandfather had cut the trees on this land, Dad said, and put up fences so that people would not keep walking across it. Grandpa had cleared this land with his brother Morris for years and then later with my father and my uncles. Because Grandpa had tamed the land, Dad said, the government sold it to him at a price he could afford.

That homeplace farm lay near a town called Trail. There the railroad crossed a path that, for hundreds of years, people had walked to get from the wild rice lakes to the berry patches and fishing lakes farther east. To the other side was a town called Gully because of the ditch down its center that had once drained a lake named Agassiz.

One clear afternoon, Grandpa idled the tractor near nine of us cousins picking chokecherries at the edge of the field; our older cousin, a boy, was already out harvesting the back forty. Time had come, Grandpa said, for us to learn to drive.

The other boys, even though they were younger than I was, got their turns on the John Deere AR first, but at last I climbed up onto the chassis.

Grandpa motioned with his chin for me to sit on the fender. "You're a girl, right?" he said. I nodded. "And the oldest of the girls?" he asked. I nodded again.

"It's time then," he said, "for you to learn why our family is registered as Heathen in Denmark." He did not give up the wheel but turned the tractor out into the corn rows.

"My father's grandfather was a Lutheran priest in the old country." He turned to me sternly: "You remember this now! I count on you to tell the others later when they want to hear."

"I will remember," I told him, glancing covetously at the wheel.

"Hans Nelson was his name. His son, my grandfather, as the eldest held the name Nels Hanson. After they came to this country, they stopped changing their surnames, so Hanson we have remained," Grandpa said. "I am happy to say that, when Hans Nelson was called by the Lord, he humbled himself and was saved. Through Scripture, God showed him that to stand between the Lord and the people would cause them to fall into idolatry. Each person must stand alone before God; no one can mediate between man and God but Jesus Christ our Lord. I trust you understand this. My great-grandfather recognized that he could no longer walk toward the pulpit in vestments and robe. So he turned to farming.

"One day," Grandpa continued, maneuvering the tractor around the end of the row, "the census taker came to the farm. He gathered statistics—how many girls, how many boys—and then lifted his pencil and said, 'Of course, you are Lutherans here.' 'Certainly not!' said my great-grandpa Nelson. 'Ah, Catholic then?' 'Not papists! Not we!' said the old man. 'Well,' said that census-taking man, 'there are only three boxes here—Lutheran, Catholic, or Heathen.'"

Like his great-grandfather before him, my grandfather paused. "Hans Nelson thought for a bit," Grandpa said, "and then he replied, 'If those are the choices we have, mark us down as Heathen!'"

Grandpa looked over toward me. "You got that?" he asked. I nodded. "If anyone asks why our family is listed as Heathen in Denmark, you are the one to explain."

We were back then where we had started. "Next!" he called to the girls.

I never learned how to drive a tractor.

Sometime later, Grandpa took me to see the new pews in a

chapel at Leech Lake Reservation. He had given money for those furnishings, maybe out of some sense of responsibility. He believed that the Indians, too, needed to be saved.

Winter

At the farms, my brothers and my cousins and I ran wild. We swung on the haymow's braided rope until the weather turned brutally cold. We built houses in the snow, crowded together in the bunk beds, told stories into the dark of the nights.

We went to church together, the farm girl cousins in patent leather shoes and crinkly skirts. With one family of cousins we went to the Baptist church, with the other to the Assembly of God. On the weekends when we went east to Bemidji, where my smaller group of cousins lived, we met with Nymore Assembly.

My parents preferred that assembly. There the people were free to minister one to another, no pastor above them. Anyone could speak from the gathered group. Anyone could suggest a song. We met on Sunday afternoons, my mom sitting with her mandolin on the platform among the other musicians.

To keep from being bored during the three-hour services, I rolled cloth babies in a cradle hankie and ate raisins one by one from a small box, but usually I was not bored. Molly, one of the elders of the assembly, would stand up at some point, her calf-length cotton dress buttoned over her ponderous breasts and wide belly. She'd lay her Bible on the back of the pew before her and open it, often to Leviticus to expound on the reasons God instructed Moses to build the Ark of the Covenant. She described the cloth hangings that Moses used to surround the tabernacle. Women probably wove those hangings, she said, though only men could enter that "holy of holies" where the ark was kept. I liked the crinkly feel of my Bible's pages as I turned them to search for the verses she read. Onionskin, Mom said that paper was called.

My elders were convinced that they were following the only dictates of God. When I was eight, I dared to stand up in meeting myself. I told the gathered folk that, because I had accepted Jesus as my savior, I was now a Christian like they were. I asked them to sing "How Great Thou Art." The adults nodded approval and turned to that page in their hymnals. Our voices boomed against the roof of the basement assembly room: "Oh, Lord my God, when I in awesome wonder, consider all the worlds Thy hands have made. I see the hills; I hear the rolling thunder . . ."

Was it God I loved or was it Life?

School had not yet captured my imagination. The discussions between my father and my uncle intrigued me far more than did Dick and Jane and that city dog Spot. I listened from blankets spread as a bed on the living room floor at the farm as Dad and Uncle Reuben debated hotly whether the Rapture would come before or after the Tribulation, comparing Bible verses that implied one with those that seemed to indicate the other.

As I drifted to sleep, I would hear the whine of the wind, the splatter of icy snow against the panes. My father and my uncle would laugh and slap their knees in delight when one of them read again the verse that said, "Every knee shall bow, every tongue shall declare, that Jesus Christ is Lord." I snuggled down into the confidence that we already knew the truth, and that, one day, everyone else—all those worldly people—would come to know it as well.

Uneasily, though, I hoped the Rapture would not come while I slept. I preferred to stay in this world. Meeting my dead uncle Morris would be nice, but I was terribly fond of my dog and she, it was claimed, would not be lifted up on high.

The earth was a bowl on which I rested. Family and religion encircled me with love, laid their words over my thoughts. Only on the margins had civilized culture and school begun to intrude.

Spring

Then we moved to the woods.

Grandma came with us the first time we visited the lake. We left the soft oaks and maples, the rolling fields and sandy lakeshores, and entered a land of tall pines. We came to a cabin at the side of a lake where loons called, where the shore was rocky. I found no smooth place to walk into the water.

My father took a job teaching shop in the town by that lake, so we moved away from the cousins. Our first house stood in town, a prefab like all the rest, but near to the woods, the only house available to us that had old trees at its back. Three moose, a mother and her two young, visited one day; we crowded out onto the back step to watch them walk past.

The next spring, men came walking down our street with cans and sprayer attachments to spew DDT over our yard. Though the mosquitoes were thick, my mother had read *Silent Spring* and ran out in protest. "Not our yard, not my children, not here!" She waved her hands at them. Laughing, they sprayed anyway.

Soon after, my dad told me to hop in the car. He drove a mile out of town, turned down a road with a grassy patch between the tire lines. Half a mile on, he pulled into a cut among the trees. I walked with him to a place where we could just see the blue lake through a break in the birches.

"Beautiful?" he asked. "I'm leasing this land. We're going to build a house halfway down the hill. Are you glad?"

I was nine. I had made a couple of friends in town. They would never walk two miles to play with me. Here was a jumble of brush and rock. No. I did not want to come here. I did not want to come here at all.

We came anyway.

Summer

Before the house, we built a Lincoln cabin. We laid spruce logs on three sides, hung a canvas tarp over the south-facing open side, and positioned a wood-burning stove to the west. There we ate and played games and told stories during the many months of house building.

My new sister lay on a blanket on the ground. My first-grade brother and I sat on tree stumps next to each other as he did his best to read, even though he saw the letters and words backward to the way they appeared to me.

Sand flies chewed off patches of our skin; our necks and hairlines would begin to itch on the second day. Mother spread calamine over them.

We picked mint to boil in water for tea. We hauled rocks, burned brush, applied bug dope, changed the baby, leveled ground. My brothers helped Dad build rock walls. I prepared food with my mom. I watched as Dad drilled down a sandpoint to get water for drinking; what he pulled up was the sweetest water any of us had ever tasted, cleaned by the pond across our road, then wiped pure by the sand and rocks and tiny creatures down where the water table fed it to us.

Only in the evenings, when I stood alone looking at the lake, did I feel lonely. My town friends had, as I had expected, faded away. I thought, *I am alone; no one has been here before us; we are the first here building this house.*

We were teachers from a farm town. The people in town were miners from other places where they had failed at being other things. They did not belong here either. Everyone that I knew was a Finn or a Slovak or a Norwegian or a German or a Pole or a Communist. There were no Americans that I ever heard of among us.

By then I had learned a history of this land. Before the taconite miners had come the high-grade ore miners; before that, the Englishmen to teach the miners to mine; before that, the Finns, who tried to farm; before that, the lumbermen; before that, the Frenchmen, who took furs. No one before. The fur trappers left cabins; the lumbermen, tree stumps; the Finns, grandmothers on swamp farms; the Englishmen, mine shafts; the miners, company towns. All of us came from somewhere else. None of us belonged.

Just the same, Dad said, we had come to stay.

I was not so sure. I wished for friends, wanted to return to my cousins.

Sometimes we attended the Baptist church in town, though my parents did not agree to the necessity of sacraments. Not only my great-great-grandfather in Denmark, but each of my parents' parents had been "saved out of Lutheranism." Dad said we were not about to return to denominational bondage, that we must affirm no authority other than Scripture and God. Such freethinking made us ill suited for any church in our town.

For a time, we were welcomed by the Baptists. One Sunday I watched my friends walk to the front, where the preacher dunked them into the water of the very clean cow trough that was usually covered with boards and a dresser scarf. They went down as heathens and came up, soaking wet, as Christians. Could I stay in Girls' Guild, would I ever get invited to birthday parties, if I did not get dunked too?

My father explained that, since I had already accepted Jesus as my savior and confessed my sins, nothing else was required of me. But had I actually confessed my sins? What sins did I have to confess? True, I had hoped that Jesus would not return very soon, but did that count? If it were truly a sin, was I required to give up that hope?

Baptism seemed easier, necessary or not, so I told my parents that I wished, like my friends, to go under the water. Dad argued against that and read the pertinent Bible passages with me. I persisted.

He acquiesced but said that he'd prefer I be baptized by the elders at Nymore Assembly than by the preacher at the Baptist church. That was good by me.

We drove three hours to Bemidji. After the meeting on Sunday afternoon, a procession of cars wove to the Mississippi. I walked in my pedal pushers, blouse, and tennis shoes with Elders Sandeen and Beckstrand over the pebbled shore and into the reeds of the river until we were waist-deep. One of them placed a handkerchief over my mouth and nose and held the back of my head. The other held my waist. Together, they dunked me backward into the river. I believe they followed my father's choice and baptized me "in the name of Jesus" instead of "in the name of the Father, the Son, and the Holy Ghost." What I remember is the cold clasp of the water over the new mounds on my chest.

On the shore, Mother handed me a towel. I hung my head, water dripping from my ponytail, and walked to the car.

It was done.

I had given myself to the river.

I glanced back once we got to the car. There it was—the place where the water began.

And then we went home. No one at the Baptist church knew, or cared, that I had been baptized.

What I had found was that I belonged in the water and in the woods.

We spent long days kneeling under red pines picking blueberries. I settled into the emptiness of bliss with moss under my knees, pine smell filling my head, bulging blue rolling into my hands.

Mom and I walked through the woods with juice cans strung on twine hanging around our necks. We filled the cans with serviceberries, pin cherries, and plums.

We scrounged the roadsides for strawberries early in the season and for rosehips as the summer turned.

When we noticed standing deadwood or recently downed trees, we dragged them back to the lot. Dad and the boys would split them while Mom and I made puddings and pies. We'd cool off after the work by jumping into the lake.

From the garden we picked beans and corn and peas.

My mother ground wheat and made bread. I blended cream to make butter and formed it into roses or squirrels before setting it, proudly, on the table.

Fall

Dad would build a fire in the woodstove downstairs. Mom and I would lay the screens taken from summer's windows over the top and spread on them peppermint and rosehips to dry for wintertime tea. The house would fill with the smells of rose and mint. We would be ready for cold.

One year, my parents, my sister, my brothers, and I attended a weeklong family Bible camp at Lake Pokegama, a swelling along a stretch of the Mississippi. A dashing, charismatic preacher from New York City led our preteen Bible class in a study of Solomon's Song. He insisted that the bawdy words were to be sung only to God, even though our rejected sexuality, like his own secret inclinations, bubbled just beneath the surface, peeping through now and again to confuse.

Early one morning we gathered in the chapel for service. The choruses began; hands were lifted in praise; the preacher told us all to stand. Some swayed side to side, others softly chanted the usual sentences in tongues—"Hallimashina"—or in English—"O Jesus, come! Dear Jesus, come!" Some squeezed past their row-mates to move to the front where the dancing in the spirit would commence.

I stood quietly in my place. My parents had pointed out Scripture verses to prove that neither speaking in tongues, nor dancing, nor even wailing and moaning in ecstasy would prove that one was a Child of God. "All that is needed," my parents said, "is belief in the sacrifice of Christ." So our family tended toward quiet.

If God was going to lead me to speaking in languages other than the one I knew, if God was going to command my feet to dance, He would have to do it directly. I would not pretend to fit in.

The preacher lifted his voice. "O Almighty!" he cried in a tenor tune. "Fill your people. Hear our cry. Bring us to the glory of Shekinah."

I shifted uncomfortably and looked to my parents' bowed heads.

The preacher's voice changed, became fierce. "I feel a spirit of oppression. There is among us a heaviness, a weight that is holding us down. O Lord! Relieve us!" He opened his eyes and scanned the small crowd, each row of folk standing in front of their raw-pine benches.

"I command you!" he shouted. "In the name of Jesus Christ of Nazareth, I command you. Be gone! Spirit of oppression, set God's people free!"

I edged past my benchmates and out the door.

The oppressor was me.

Walking through the ferns and fallen pine needles, I noticed that, yes, the keening had risen in fervor after my departure.

I leaned against the rusty medallions of a red pine's bark and then slid to the ground in a mossy green clearing.

In my heart I accepted this verdict: I was outside the circle of good. I was not one of God's folk.

If divinity did not move inside me, I was an outcast; the others were the chosen.

Then I heard a sentence, the words arriving clearly into my mind.

"You know God," those words said.

I opened my eyes, alert.

Beyond the mottled red trunks of the trees, behind the soft fronds of the white pines and the bunching tufts of the reds, light danced over the blue of the lake. A breath of wind caught my hair and the strands of grasses nearby.

That was the first time Earth deigned to speak, plainly in English. And I heard.

Winter

Later in the fall, walking the two miles home from school down our dirt road through the maples and birches and pines, I noticed my legs moving beneath me. By this time, I had come to love school. Though I had few friends, the teachers liked me. I was quick, they said. I enjoyed doing math, liked writing, read eagerly once there was more to it than Dick and Jane and that silly dog. But that day, I noticed that the teachers' praise was all for my head. I wondered if my body and legs had any use. *Maybe,* I thought, *I should be just a head, pulled about on a cart.*

That did not seem right. Since I had a body, since there were these trees and that deer and this birdsong surrounding me, it seemed I should not be a thought machine performing at school.

My Latin teacher had given us the task of memorizing scientific names for regional trees around us. I decided I would learn not only their names but also the shapes of their leaves. I would begin, again, to walk among them.

And so I did. After Grandma died, my grandfather had come to stay with us. During those months, he had made rough paths through the underbrush in the woods. One path passed by a huge glacier-dropped rock. We children had picnicked on that boulder in summer, watched a bear amble past. The boys had camped in its craggy opening. I practiced following that path the quarter mile to the rock, memorizing the places where it nearly disappeared into hazel brush.

Then, near winter, Dad challenged me to get to the rock alone after dark. I wore moccasins to feel the firmer ground where the path lay. Twice I lost my way, but each time I found the path again, trusting my eyes if I softened them and looked only through their edges. Any bear, I knew, would smell and be frightened by me. Without a flashlight, I had learned, I could see more than with one and, importantly, I could see without being seen.

The winters came cold. Crisp cold. Mom and I walked out on the lake, thinking to cross to the nearest island. We had nearly made it to Lightning Island when we remembered we had not turned back to test the going-home wind. We turned and felt the wind rip between the buttons on our coats. We would not be able to get to even that close island, not if we had to walk home afterward in the wind, so we crossed our arms in front of us and made for home.

We got home, passing a fox on the way, our wool scarves frozen over our mouths, our eyelashes heavy with ice, our hands numb in our mitts. Never again did Mother or I forget to turn to test the wind before heading off across the lake.

Later that night, warming myself in a bath, I wondered how the fox would get warm. Did it wish for a bath after its trek over the lake? I had hot water; it did not. I doubted it had forgotten to turn its nose into the wind.

Saturday nights we drove to family friends, woods people who were outsiders like we were. They lived on a lowland by a small creek. In the loosely connected, fiercely independent, unaffiliated Christian network of the north, we kids found few friends of whom our parents fully approved. The two sisters in the family and I were lucky that, for a good many years, our parents got along.

My friends' yard smelled sweetly of wood chips trodden down on the path from the woodshed to the sauna. Smoke rose cleanly from the sauna into the cold still air where the moon tore away from the tangle of birch twigs frozen against the sky.

We girls took sauna first. A crack of icy night came through the bathhouse window to where we washed our hair. After sauna we jumped into the snow and then ran back to the heat.

The house smelled of woodstove-baked bread, apple crisp, and jam. After the boys came in from their bath, we poured mugs of hot cider and played Dutch Blitz by the light of kerosene lamps.

In their barn was the brown heifer that we fed with molasses and oats. We scratched between her ears and leaned against her warm sides, this friend we would eat the next fall.

Some weekends, my two friends and I went winter camping. We'd drag supplies on a sled several miles into the woods until we'd arrive at a trapper's cabin called Kalastus Järvi—Finnish for "fishing lakes." Always there would be chopped wood alongside the cabin, tinned food on the shelves. We'd use the wood and eat the food and then leave behind us wood that we chopped and tins of food that we brought. On the walls were calendars of women in bathing suits; in the nights mice nibbled at the quilts under which we slept.

We were, mostly, at peace.

At home by the lake, I walked out alone into the dark. The snow squeaked under my boots in the silence of forty below. No birds in that night. No bear. No deer. The lake groaned fiercely now and again in its sleep. Somewhere a wolf was making tracks across it, silent as the moon, thin as a birch shadow.

I walked to the pond. The sound of distant trucks wandered over the miles from the mine, down from the hill, to trouble the silence of the woods, of the snow, of my stiff boots and my numb fingers curled whitely into the palms of my gloves.

Spring

The woods had caught me; the trees taught me lessons; the wolves had sung to me. I became known to my place on earth; I let my feet grow into the shallow soil, found nurturing cracks in the rocks. My hair was pollinated by the wind. I became part of the land. Like most others, I arrived foreign, but slowly I became earth.

In early spring, water formed new rivulets out of each bank of snow. The snow would be deep and white, the water clear and cold. I washed my boot bottoms in the running streams. The edges of the snowbanks curled back to reveal trails on which small animals had run all winter, safe beneath a covering of snow.

In our town, snow that melts and rain that falls washes into the creek behind the high school and flows with it to the Embarrass River. That river moves on to join the St. Louis and out to Lake

17

Superior. However, if our rainfall and snowmelt sink deeply enough into the ground, they join the water table that flows north to the edges of the lake where we live. Springs seep out just above lake level. Joining the lake, the water flows east to meet the Kawishiwi River, then the White Iron Chain of Lakes, and, at land's end, Hudson Bay. When snow clings to the top of our car and then drops off after the ridge forty-five miles west, it runs south to join the Mississippi.

This swampy land divides the waters. In spring, I would watch the water set out.

As the weather warmed, I'd return to the pond. First, I would go wrapped in my coat and a blanket. The pond, called Minnow Lake on local maps, is kidney shaped, made up of two bays that connect down the middle. Loons shouldn't land there. Once I watched a loon walk awkwardly across the road from the pond to the lake, unable to become airborne after landing on so small a surface. It almost fell on its chest as it crossed the road because its legs were too far back to balance its weight. The turtles I met fared better; they could walk across the road to either side and find a place to swim.

I would curl myself into the body-sized nook at the top of a rock that rose just off the shore of the pond, and I would read. Mallards would swim by me in pairs. Dragonflies would land. Sometimes, looking up from a page, I'd see a beaver's head and tail across the other bay. Deer would come to drink by the far shore. Blackbirds would sing. Mergansers would settle down.

Some days I'd hike to the far side and read under the birches. I planned to build my house, one day, beyond the swampy inlet where pines crowned the rise.

At the pond I read novels by women—the Brontës, Alcott, Austen. For school I read the acknowledged great men, but at the pond, women were allowed.

Back near the shore below the house in evening, fireflies blinked through the valley. Frogs called.

One late spring, the breeze beckoned me out. I rose in the night, wrapped in a blanket, and went out onto the moonlit grass. I lay with the blanket over both me and the earth. Wind soughed through the pines that grew near. Loons wailed across the lake. I was at home.

Summer

Summer was for entering the roadless lands. While I was young, the waters between us and Canada were wild and free. We went into them when we pleased, traveled as long as we liked.

I went canoe camping with the two sisters who were my friends. Others came to our woods as well. Sometimes on the portages, we met those tourists. They stepped aside when they saw three girls carrying a canoe across, two of us in skirts, our cotton shirts and old shoes dirty from swamp muck and campfire soot. We were shy; we were proud. We picked sites as far as possible from other campers so that, mostly, we could be alone—alone in the mist-shrouded mornings with loons. Alone for afternoon baths in whirlpool streams that tumbled from one lake to the next. We cooked our meals in tinfoil and drank wintergreen tea in silence. We were alone for our evening swims, naked before bed.

Other times, my whole family pushed out in canoes and then set up camp far down the river. I would wake with the dew-wet roof of the tent tightening in the sun. Outside, early light would skim along the surface of the lake, trailing over the tracks of two water bugs, gleaming off the flatness. In the trees, light would catch drops that clung on spider threads, and I would see, briefly, how closely I was held in a compassing net of myriad circling webs. This was morning, morning at the lake. I would kneel on a rock and, cupping my hands, wash myself with the water.

In the midafternoon, camp broken for the day, the older of my brothers and I paddled the lead canoe, my dad and younger brother following in the next. We rounded a bend in the Kawishiwi and saw, there, on the flat rock bluff that was, season by season, chipping off into the river, pictures painted into the rocks.

I had not known they would be there. Red paintings of deer and humans, of something like a canoe and a bear. My brother and I gazed in silence.

Others had been in this watershed before us. Until then, I had not realized this. Until then, I had thought we were the first.

But these paintings spoke of long knowledge. What those others had painted I had begun to learn by walking silently without shoes or light through the night woods. They knew what the swamp-red waters could teach. They had heard what the night-flying squirrels might say. They had left a sign.

At sixteen I traveled by car with family friends from Minnesota to New York City and then to Washington, D.C.—my first trip east.

We set out toward Chicago, then through it, into Indiana and Pennsylvania. There, a panic rose in me.

Nowhere was open space. Everything along the highway was fenced. I could not fathom where people walked. At home, I could slip out the kitchen door, climb the stone steps, cross the dirt road, and enter the woods. I could walk the whole day without meeting a person or encountering a fence. Along this eastern highway, everything was private, all the edges claimed.

In Greenwich Village we slept in armchairs at the home of Zoot, a famous saxophonist whom I had never heard of. In Maryland I attended my host family's son's wedding, drank wine, and tried not to sway with the jazz. At the Smithsonian we peered into a space capsule.

Then, on a street in Washington, D.C., someone asked me where I was from. "Minnesota," I told him.

"Minnesota!" he echoed back. "You still killing Indians there?"

I hadn't known. Had we in Minnesota killed one another?

Fall

It wasn't that I didn't know violence. I had walked home one day from babysitting a small boy who had kicked through the window when I tried to take him off the kitchen table. I walked away from that house, hearing first the wind in the poplar leaves, then the smack of the two-by-four as the boy's father began beating him.

On another day, a neighbor woman had knocked at our door, desperate to keep her baby alive. My mother went home with her, saw the dehydrated infant, and said it had to be taken to the doctor. Its father said, no, the mother would have to care for it herself. My mom showed her how to soak a cotton ball in breast milk and water and put that under the dry baby's tongue. It did not rebound.

At last the father laid his baby in the car, told the mother to stay home, and drove with the child toward the hospital. When he arrived, the baby was dead.

Mom and I did not know what to do. We spoke together in whispers.

There was other violence, too, though I heard details only years later. Children beaten, schoolboys breaking other children's noses, mothers thrashed, boys and girls seduced and raped, young ones repeatedly pounded.

Winter

Before I left home for college, I heard that sulfide ores had been discovered at the outlet of our lake where the waters fed into the Kawishiwi. We had learned about taconite mines at school and on annual tours. Once a year, buses filled with us townfolk had climbed the hill along the south side of town so that we could look into the pit. We watched the crusher grind the rock as workers in hard hats explained the process and its benefits. The first time we went, they said that the ore would last ninety-nine years, long enough to keep us all fed.

I was taken aback by the immense gouges into the land. Topsoil and birches and cougars were gone. Butterflies and grosbeaks. Everyone gone. The tour guide pointed toward drills melting holes into the base of the pit. He motioned toward raw sections of rock that had been cracked apart by the latest Wednesday and Saturday blasts, the ones that had shaken our school desks and houses. He showed us trucks with tires taller than a car and cranes dumping blasted rock into the massive beds.

Maybe this mine was needed. We all drove cars, didn't we?

In elementary school I had learned which resources came from which places. From our place came timber and ore, also wild rice and fish.

The rocks and trees, the fish and the plants seemed to me to be the place itself. How could a place exist if its parts were taken away?

If the mining ended—and, before long, that day seemed to be approaching more quickly than ninety-nine years—perhaps the soil would rebuild, the wilder animals return. But that hole on the hill inspired awe with its size. Could it just crust over? And what would become of the workers?

Sulfide mining, my family learned, would be something even bigger than taconite. For one thing, it would be closer. The ore seam extended under our lake, probably also into lands farther north where no one had yet been allowed to drill test holes. Those were waters into which we dipped our cups over the side of the canoe, waters we drank without boiling. There we had watched otters play. One morning, looking from my tent, I had seen the head of a buck as it swam across the lake. There, often, we had outwitted bear. We had watched mink, had seen snakes slither past. The mine would settle between us and all that.

More shocking was this: sulfide mining was said to permanently damage the waters it touched.

* * *

I left those rugged waters for college because I wanted to under-stand the world. The campus I went to in the south of the state sat above rolling, field-covered hills. A river flowed far below in a tamed valley. I would stand on the hill in front of Old Main, looking toward the river, feeling uneasy and exposed in the soft openness.

I felt foreign compared to the other students, who drank beer and walked out of class to protest the Vietnam War. I admired the protesters, but I preferred to go to class.

As a college community, we read *The Greening of America. My woods*, I thought, *were already green.* I studied my classmates as they spoke through megaphones and pitched tents on the quad; I would need to know how to do the same when the day came that I'd be called to lay my body in front of bulldozers at the headwaters of the Kawishiwi.

That day did not arrive. Talk of sulfide mining in Minnesota faded; cheaper ore could be taken from the center of Africa. I did not ask—did not think—about the lands and people of Africa. I was glad that the river I knew was at peace.

Most summers I'd go back to the lake. I'd sink my feet again into that watery world. When I walked down the moss-covered wooden slat steps toward the lake, I'd see water seeping from the sides of the hill. It would soak in the humus and coalesce into streams. In some patches it would make of the soil a boggy marsh that would suck the boot right off my foot. With the water, I'd make my way to the lake. There the streams would meet the water's expanse and I would find myself, my face reflected up from the lake's surface.

By winter, I'd be out again in the world, not as sinful a world as I had been led to expect.

I found a friend in a girl from Rockford who also liked to study. She was black. My African American great-aunt had played man-dolin on the platform with Mom, and Brother Sadler had come to our house to preach; one black boy from Chicago had washed dishes next to me at Bible camp. But I had never before known a black girl my age. She was more like me than were the evangelicals—quiet and reserved in her faith.

* * *

I still sometimes tried to speak as the fundamentalists did, saying "Thank the Lord" and "God bless you," and bowing my head before meals. But I was finding that Buber and Tillich and Niebuhr, the men whose words I read in religion class, made more sense to me. They spoke shockingly of "The Death of God" but then explained how, through a symbolic death, even through the death of Jesus, divinity had enlivened the All. They considered God in-earthed.

As a junior, I flew to northern England to stay in Europe for a year. Traveling for the first time by airplane, I saw the ocean from the sky, broad and reaching.

That decade saw a sexual revolution in the United States and Europe, a raucous breaking loose in which I did not wish to participate.

That year, 1970, was in the middle of the U.S. war in Vietnam. Over the BBC we heard about the killings at Kent State and Jackson State.

Yet, in Durham, England, what met me was beauty. As I walked stone alleys past the castle, heard bells ring quarter hours from the cathedral, saw larks, I recognized places that I had met in writing by Shakespeare, the Brontës, and Hardy. Literature, I had unconsciously assumed, took place in fictional lands. My land and I had never been part of the history I learned, not part of the literature I read. But here I saw that other people wrote about places they actually lived in, places that still were alive—lands that seethed with history.

I also discovered, to my surprise, that some people found my life interesting. My new friends had never been in a canoe, did not know how to knead bread, had not built a fire or slept in a tent. They could do other things—dance, drink sherry, prune roses. They all had heard of Cézanne

24

One of them came from Cape Cod. She wore hats and spoke like the Kennedys.

She also was afraid she might be lesbian. My family training told me that she wasn't. No one, I had been assured, actually *was*, though some were misled into thinking they might be.

I thought back to that summer camp preacher from New York City—a year after camp he had confessed to his wife and the congregation about his affair with the man whom he mentored. Both the men had been quickly forgiven, redeemed, and embraced.

So, on a footbridge over the River Wear with trees from a Turner painting bowing over us and matins bells ringing from the clock tower, I told my friend to relax. God, I said, would take care of the problem. And her love for me? That was natural, I said. My cousins loved me and I them. My friends loved me. We shared beds. We hugged. This was nothing, I said, out of the ordinary.

"Could I kiss you?" she asked.

May all be as lucky as I, to be kissed for the first time on the banks of a river in England with nightingales beginning to sing.

My friend and I checked the encyclopedia at our college and read that lesbianism was "a mental illness, considered incurable, especially for the more masculine women." In addition, it was illegal; if one tried to immigrate to the United States with such a "condition," she would not be allowed in. The encyclopedia did not explain, though, exactly what action or feeling turned one into such a woman.

My friend had gray-green eyes. When she laughed, the corners around them crinkled. She did not laugh often, her fate weighing heavily upon her. She sensed no God standing with her; therefore, I was determined that I would stay by her.

At Christmas I sailed by ship to Norway. When, the morning we landed, I stood on the deck and saw rocks rising like obelisks up out of the sea, I felt I had always known this scene. I was coming home, home to the place my maternal grandfather had left, home to a place deeply etched into my bones. Though I had always called myself Norwegian—such was my identity in my hometown—I had not known that this scene of rocks rising from ocean flowed beneath in my blood.

Then I met Norwegian young people, acquaintances of my two sister-friends from back home, and learned that I could not be Norwegian, no matter how I felt when I saw that shore. My new Norwegian companions asked me why I was bombing Cambodia. I objected. I was not bombing anyone.

The next week, traveling through Germany and Holland, I tried to pass as a student from England. My identity had become complex.

During spring break we traveled by boat to Mykonos in Greece. There we swam in the blue of the Mediterranean. As I stood on the deck of the steamer returning to Athens, I recognized that the blue of that sea was implanting itself in my soul with an urgency I did not understand.

The atmospheric CO_2 levels in 1970 were 325.54 parts per million. I did not know then that these numbers mattered. I recognized the world as a paradise. I did not know that my flying above it, steaming through it, and eating eagerly of it were partaking in its destruction. I knew that, in my north woods, the soil lay thin and delicate over the rock base. I assumed that the rest of the land was staunch and would be, forever, as it was then.

That year the human population was 3.7 billion, a sustainable number. The ocean pH was still safe for coral, the sea free of plastic. In England, people carried groceries home from the market in woven string bags.

By 1980, the atmospheric CO_2 was 338.09, up 12.55 from ten years before. The human weight on the earth was 4.54 billion, nearly a billion additional people. There were more of us than the land and sea could provide for long term. We humans had begun to bring our groceries home in plastic. I missed the string bags, did not know anything about CO_2, and flew three times back to

Europe. Like almost everyone else, I was unaware of which actions mattered most.

In the mid-1980s, at a college in west-central Minnesota where I taught, I leaned back in my desk chair one day, stunned by the words of a radio announcer. He said that our industrialized way of life was causing Minnesota to become an increasingly cloudy state. The decrease in sunny blue days, the announcer said, was being blamed for a marked increase in winter depression.

Spring

I returned often to the woods of my home in the north. As I did the daily chores—washing dishes, sweeping the floor, setting out a meal, hanging clothes—I would glance without conscious thought toward the lake. It spread white in the mornings, azure with reflected clouds in the midday, a ruffled turquoise in afternoon. It lay like fierce steel before a storm, silver stretching past the green of the opposite shore to meet the silver of sky on a cloudy evening, or pink and powder blue at bedtime. In the night when I woke and looked out, it would be silent indigo or fiercely tossed with white-tipped waves or, on nights of no moon, present only in its invisibility.

Life was the point of Life. God was a paddle dipped into the lake. God was in the loon and in the blueberry plant.

Handholds and Stepping-Stones

When nearing the shore from a canoe,
eye the land carefully to choose the best
branch to grab and the most stable rock
on which to plant a first foot.

While walking through the woods at night,
carry a stick to test the ground ahead for
firm patches of path, to warn of mucky
holes and dropping-away edges.

* * *

When in distress, grab hold of these rungs first:

Stop

Breathe

Listen

Feel

Connect

Witness

Walk

Nourish

Rest

Be

When you are able to act,
move to these firm stones:

Survey the scene.

Follow cycles of activity.

Settle into the soil and its wisdom.

Grieve with containment and love.

Humbly value all efforts.

Retell stories, both the painful and the hopeful.

Nourish other lives with your energies.

Plant and water and make soil;
find your nearest watershed.

Allow for possibilities, dreaming,
mystery, and the unknown.

Leave gently when death arrives.

2

DO NOT FALL AWAY

During graduate school in Ohio, I began to see the woods where I had grown up as an outsider would. I had thought we were living a real-time regular life, that eating from the woods was what people did.

But the lakes I had canoed on were now a designated and protected wilderness. People could no longer simply put in and paddle; now visitors and residents alike had to apply for a permit, enter a predetermined lake, follow designated portages, stop at official sites, and leave after the number of days allowed.

From the distance of Ohio and graduate school, I saw my earlier life as a natural history museum tableau. We had been living the past. We had been part of nature. We were expected, like that Indian man at the Mississippi headwaters, to fade politely away.

* . * . *

Gradually during my twenties and early thirties, I made a path for myself into an urban world. I began to piece together community and meaning in a city even though its parks did not feel like nature to me. People might appear on any turn of a rustic path. I knew there were no bears nearby. Airplanes roared above the trees; siren howls drowned out birdsongs. I attempted to find a way of life without my woods.

Eventually, I rented a house by the shores of Lake Pepin, a bulge in the flow of the Mississippi, fifty miles south of the city. I could be there half of each week and still hold down a job in town. Though that landscape rolled more gently than the woods up north, my soul began to settle. Morel mushrooms sprang forth in spring. Corn and beans and squash plumped long before vines had begun to fruit in our Northwoods garden. Gullies filled with oak trees threaded through the rolling fields. Streams flowed down the valleys toward the wide-spreading lake below. My house sat in a yard shushed by fir trees and near to a gulch of hardwoods where trillium bloomed in spring.

I needed to know this land more directly, so I took my small dog and a sleeping bag and walked into the lowland one evening. We found a well-hidden dip and settled down with the night.

I didn't sleep much, being cold and slightly afraid that people might happen into those woods.

Sometime in the night, Earth spoke: "Now is the time. We are sending children to you."

Soon after, I became pregnant.

*   *   *

My children's father and I were not yet married. My parents, my uncles and aunts—all were shamed by this. "We once had," my uncle told me, "such hopes for you."

"The day you told me you were pregnant," my mother wrote, "was the worst day of my life." My break from the family creed had become public.

*   *   *

And yet—I had the lake.

One week my baby and I returned to the house in the north

alone. First thing each morning and last thing each night, we stood at the end of the dock to speak with the water and sky. We slept to the sounds of the loons and woke to the dew on the grass.

On a night of half-moon, I went down to the water alone. I paddled out, a monitor with the sound of the baby's quiet breathing lying on the floor of the canoe. A bat swung over the boat. Full out in the bay, loons called. The moon rose from the trees as I paddled, and the black water splashed on the sides. I saw no lights on the stretch of the shore, only the points of the stars.

And then, with the moon above and the cooling breeze around, I took off my clothes and lowered myself over the side of the boat.

I swam—all of me under the black of the water. There were bats above, gulls sleeping on rocks with their heads under their wings, loons gliding together. Under the water were fishes, strange and dark and weaving. And I was there, free to give myself to this lake.

*   *   *

In the summer of 1989, the rains did not come. They continued not to come.

Leaves withered and fell from the trees in June.

My son was two years old. I was awaiting a second child.

The dry skies unsettled me. We lived then in the city with my children's father and his daughter and a swirling gaggle of friends. None of those friends seemed to be ripped open by the drought the way I was.

I put my child in a red wagon and surrounded him with jugs of water; we walked up and down the sidewalk, pouring water on the trees.

I heard about El Niño. And then some hints of climate change.

When I drove north, I noticed that the pines on the southern edge of the boreal forest were dying. On the slope from the house to the lake, the birch leaves yellowed and branches fell. Tent caterpillars ate young leaves as they sprouted on the trees. The mink abandoned the shore.

Could humans, in a mass, truly doom life?

I had brought two more to this land.

* * *

Daily life consumed my time. The needs of my children filled my mind. My attempts to partner dissolved into disaster. Responsible for the financial and daily survival of the children, I worked toward a doctorate while teaching at three different colleges.

Fear of homelessness sidelined my fear of ecosystem collapse.

* * *

Sit in an overstuffed chair. Pull a toddler onto your lap. Have a kindergartner snuggle under your arm. Turn the pages of a picture book; read the words. The children will point at the pictures. They will laugh. They will jostle their legs against yours. They will lay angel hair against your arm. One of them will say, "I know I came from you, Mama, and that you came from Grandma, but where did the first person come from?"

You will recognize then and forever that these children belong to this earth. That soil and water must be sustained for them.

When, in the night, you realize that climate change means that the loons will probably die and the pines will fall into the lake, when you think that it would be wise to take these children and end things quickly, maybe by driving into that lake—you know, and continue to know, that they must live as long as they can, that you must work as hard as you can to reestablish thriving life networks.

* * *

I took my children back to the lake. We pushed down a path to the place where a spring gushes out under cedars to send its water winding through mossy, mushroom-studded banks. We went to the V-shaped trough that channels that water over logs, past rocks and eddying pools. My son pulled spruce twigs from young trees and set them into the flow. As their pitch reacted against the water, they spun like tiny mad boats toward the lake. He laughed and pulled down another pitch boat.

"Josiah," I said, "ask the tree. See if it wants so many boughs broken."

"Trees don't talk," said my son.

"Ask anyway," I told him.

He turned to the tree. His lips moved. He looked back at me. "It said 'okay,'" he assured me and ripped off yet another twig.

The next time, he paused before reaching up. His lips moved again, and then he turned to me in dismay. "Mom!" he cried out. "It said 'no.'"

We walked to the end of the trough and watched the water spill into the lake.

*   *   *

Winter was hardest. We tried to go back, though my parents had begun a cold-season migration to parts south. Dad thought that when he left he should shut off the water, drain the heat runs, stuff the chimney. We could go there, but we would be cold and we would have to pee in the snow.

I tried. The children complained.

Mostly, the snow blew there without us. When it fell at all. I listened to weather reports and worried. In the city, sometimes, winter came late, or it came all at once and then went away. Some years, winter was as winter should be. Other years, not. I read the science and worried some more.

3

PAUSE TO SURVEY

A grandfather from North Minneapolis leaned against my door-frame, halfway into the office, halfway in the hall. Richard spoke slowly, nodding his head. "What I don't get"—he paused— "is who stops the U.S. There's these laws to protect the earth. And we're breaking them. I always thought . . . always thought there was someone in charge."

After a while, I said, "There's only you and me and the rest of the folk."

"Yeah," he said. "I don't think it's in me."

Then he pulled away from the wall and stood solidly on his feet. "I get it though, Miss Ranae," he said. "We really are all we got."

* * *

In the early weeks of an ethics class, my students and I wrestled with hypothetical scenarios. For example, imagine that you visit some despot-ruled city. You see ten people lined up against a wall while a man with a rifle blusters before them. Courageously, you ask the man what the problem might be. He tells you that someone related to these folks has stolen his car and that he plans to send a message to the thief by shooting all ten. "However," he says, "I'll make you a deal. You shoot one of them, and the other nine can go free."

The question we considered was: what should you do?

We focused on the reasoning and feelings that would lead us to action. Each of the students chose a respectable ethical principle, yet they came to differing actions. Some students decided that they would never kill an innocent human. Others decided that they would kill one person to save the lives of nine. Yet others objected that they would decide only when a real crisis presented itself.

A month later, a stranger with a gym bag walked into our classroom. My students were working together in groups. The man bent to unzip his bag, and then he pulled out a gun. He snapped the two parts together and panned it across the room from left to right.

We all stopped in our places.

The room had one door, and the stranger stood just inside it. A narrow band of window edged the door. The room had no computers, no emergency alarms. In those days no one carried a cell phone.

The man made a request, "All of you please leave, except for Ricardo Sanchez." A silent second slipped by as I thought: *My classroom. No one messes with my plans. No one kills my students.*

Some students got up and moved toward the door; others simply stood. A few stayed frozen in their chairs.

Ricardo stepped toward the man.

"We'll leave," I said, "but we'll take Ricardo with us."

"You the teacher?" he asked me.

"I am." A student named Mark moved behind him. Ricardo took one step nearer.

"Then you can stay, too," he said. "The rest of you get out. Ric, stay."

My children came to my mind. *Three and six,* I thought, *are bad ages to hear that your mother has been shot. But they are also not good ages to learn that your mother has abandoned her student.*

Mark grabbed the man's arms, Ricardo jumped in his face; a

woman kicked his crotch; another guy and a girl piled on top. I wrapped my hands around the barrel of the gun he held.

I remember watching legs pass in front of the muzzle. I hoped his fingers were not on the trigger.

The gun remained quiet. We wrestled the man to the floor, found handcuffs in his pockets, and cuffed his hands behind his back. I asked someone to break apart the gun and drop its contents onto the floor.

A few students still sat, merged with their chairs.

*　　*　　*

Later that day, I sat behind a door labeled Homicide at the police station downtown. An officer berated me for my actions. "You should always," he said, "do what a gunman requests.

"If he had shot even once," the policeman explained, "the bricks in those walls would have shattered; the ricocheting bits would have hit your students like bullets."

I hadn't known that. I had assessed the situation in the moment, done what seemed right to me, and no one had been hurt.

Now, though, knowing about shattering walls, I have to take them into account.

*　　*　　*

By the next class period, some students had written wills; some had arranged to spend more time with their children. I had adjusted the material of the class so that we could reflect on what had happened before moving on.

We processed our decisions and actions. Only those students who had frozen exhibited serious distress.

Those who had left the classroom managed well, whether they left thinking, *This is not my drama; I'm out of here,* or *I don't have a will that provides for my child,* or *I'll get help.*

Those who had worked together to restrain the man also did okay. "We did what had to be done," they said. "We were lucky it turned out how it did."

Mark, who had first grabbed the arms of the gunman, later explained to the class what had led to his actions: "Some years back, when I was a night janitor, I heard reports of a gunman who came into a women's college up in Canada. He lined everyone up, told the men to get out, and, after they left, shot the women one by one. I thought about that scene night after night as I swept. I vowed that I'd never be a man who would leave. I'd die if I had to, but I'd never leave."

Slowly, the more traumatized students also settled. "Next time I'm just going to run," some said. Others said, "I'll stand my ground; I'll be like Mark next time." A few said, "I'll probably panic again, but I can accept that."

*　*　*

Five of my students and I were served subpoenas to show up for depositions. We were told to save a week of the summer for court. Once we were deposed, we were not to talk to each other again, probably for fear that we would collude and change our stories.

We had become a community. But from then on, when we passed in the halls, we had to act as if we didn't know one another.

When my time came to testify, I took the stand and affirmed that I would tell the truth.

"Is this the gun that was brought into your class?" a lawyer asked me, pointing to a labeled device on the table before me.

"It's a gun," I said. "I gave the police the one that was in our class. They took the bullets, too. I don't know guns. I hope you kept track of the one we gave you."

"Just answer the question, please," said the judge.

"Do you recognize the man in the defendant's chair? Did he come into your class on the aforementioned day?"

I looked at him.

"I don't know. He could be. The man was about that tall. We handed the man to—"

"Ma'am, just answer the questions, if you please."

"I don't know."

The judge called an intermission. Everyone left except for the defendant (who didn't look at me), a guard (who stood in the doorway talking to someone else in the hall), the gun (still on that table before me), my sister, and me. I didn't know if, once a witness is sworn in, she is allowed to go find a restroom.

The man was convicted and sent back to prison. He had come after Ricardo, we were told, because he was imprisoned the first time based on Ric's testimony. He went back based on ours.

*   *   *

In summer, my kids and I visited my sister and her family in Arizona. We mothers were determined to show our children adventure, so we took the four kids to walk down a riverbed. We brought a raft to let them ride on if the water in the stream was high enough.

When we got to the stream, we saw more water than we had expected. We were happy that the kids would be able to float. Neither my sister nor I had heard the radio report of a storm breaking over the mountains the night before.

My daughter, my son, my niece, and I got onto the rubber raft. My sister and her young son waved us off, then drove a mile farther along the creek toward the place where we would join them.

The water was blue green below us, the desert brush green and brown to the sides. The three kids chattered and laughed. Our hands paddled the water along.

Suddenly, I felt a push from behind. Wilder water gushed down the creek bed and caught us. Our raft dashed toward a bramble of bushes. "Hold tight," I called to the kids, but already we were snagged. Our raft was bending. And then I was under the water.

Holding to the raft, I pulled myself up. I saw my niece floating down the stream, head aloft. My son clung to a branch upstream, yelling. I could see my daughter nowhere. I went down to get her.

Mia had been behind me on the raft, so I pushed against the

current, eyes open to the green-gray rumble of water. I kicked, I grabbed. I scrabbled for the bottom, seeking rocks, anything to pull myself toward her. I found no way forward.

I tried to rise up for a breath of air, planning to come down again, but I could not go up. Something had fixed me to the creek bed.

My lungs were empty. *I must be drowning*, I thought. This seemed to me a better option than leaving without my child. If my daughter was down there to die, I wanted to stay near her. I relaxed against the creek floor.

Next I knew, I had popped to the surface. The current swept me around the next bend, and I saw my daughter. She sat on a rock by the shore. My son also, and my niece—all three sat on the rocks.

That night I vomited brown water. My daughter asked why I had stayed down so long. I told her that I hadn't wanted to come up since I thought she was still deep in the river.

"Mom," said Mia to me, "what you did was wrong. Even if I died, you should keep living."

* * *

That fall, I signed on to teach a writing class in a maximum security prison that was mostly underground. To get to my classroom, I had to go through a series of four metal doors and two holding tanks with intercoms. Then I had to press my fingers onto a machine that would identify me before it would open a door into the teaching area.

The class was college composition. One man, John, was big, muscled, tattooed, and foreboding. And yet, somehow, gentle.

He wrote that he had grown up in Florida. For pay, he and his siblings had picked his uncle's cotton bolls clean. "Until one noonday," he wrote, "when my uncle came to our house, excited to tell us that he'd been able to buy an automated cotton gin. We tried to smile, but what we knew was that we had just lost our income. With that cotton gin, he wouldn't need us."

John had gone to jail the first time for stealing food for his brothers and sisters. In prison he was witness to a murder. After that, he said, he knew he was not safe outside the tank. A price was upon his head. So, each time out, he found a way back in.

In all, he wrote, he had seen four murders in prison, and each one meant he would be targeted anytime he got out.

"Now," he wrote, "I always refuse parole. Or I find a way not to be offered it."

In one descriptive essay, John taught me the safe toileting behavior that I'd have to employ if I were ever to be locked up. If you're wearing pants, he explained, and need to take a shit (or a pee if you're a woman), you've got to take one leg out of your pants first because most murders occur when the victim is on the can, and most could have been avoided if that person had been able to run. "You can't run," John explained, "if you've got your drawers around your knees."

During one class period, the guard called over the intercom, "Hanson! To the control booth." I ignored it; he couldn't be ordering *me*. I was busy encouraging discussion among groups of the students.

The voice came again and the guys tipped their chins to me. "You, teacher—you better go. The guard is calling you."

"Hanson," the guard said when I complied, "you stay to the front of the room. You were moving around in there, getting your back to some of the guys. You keep to the front of the room!"

That day the men asked for my story, and I told them about the guy with the gun who had messed with my class.

"You stayed there after he ordered you to leave?" asked John.

"Yes, I did," I said.

"You got kids?" he asked.

"I do."

"Teacher, you were totally wrong," he said. "You're a mother. You have a duty. You should have been out of there! Who you think would cover your kids?"

"But there was my student to consider," I said. "He probably would have died."

"You didn't give birth to that student. You gave birth to your kids. Lady, you were so wrong." He said it sadly that time, shaking his head.

"I think," I told him, "that there might be something more important than staying alive."

* * *

The last week of the class, John showed me the prison newspaper. He was its editor. The paper had won a national prize as the best prison paper in the country.

A year later he sent another issue.

And then, sometime after, I got a letter from him. He wrote that he had accepted parole. He said that our conversation had slowly altered his thinking. He was going to go out, he said, to live as a free man no matter how few those free days might be. "There are, I've come to see," he wrote, "things more important than staying alive."

Consider the Need to Stop

How, in throes of crisis, can you pause?

How, in the midst of adventure, can
you remember to survey the surroundings
for both danger and possibility?

Once you notice a danger, how will you respond?

When might you choose to give up?

What is more important than your ongoing life?

4

THE PATTERN OF BREATH

For decades, my dad recorded the temperature and weather conditions at the lake in his journal. He had only three lines available each day, but into those he also squeezed the kilowatt hours of electricity used that day and the cost of oil and gas.

One year, he discovered a manufacturer of an inflatable solar heater, so he bought one and installed it on the roof. He chuckled with delight when the heater poured sun-warmed air into the house. Before long, the plastic degraded. He gave up the heater in disgust.

In the late 1990s, the January temperatures Dad recorded puzzled him. The first week of January had always been colder. Forty below at least. Spit froze before hitting the ground then, so we could tell, even without looking at the thermometer, that the cold spell had begun. Fifty below was expected. Once the deep cold came, it used to stick around. The lake would freeze deeply and let invasive stuff die. Pests in trees would perish. Moose, we knew, loved the cold.

But the deep cold had stopped reliably arriving.

Already in the 1990s, winter was fading in our woods.

*   *   *

Traveling on the water taught me that, in a canoe, the best way to face a storm is head-on. Try to run from it and you won't know what's coming when the big waves hit. Get sideways to it and you're sure to be swamped. Head-on, eyes open, you just might survive.

*   *   *

Our life had been guided by the seasons. The frozen pole in the north had held the weathers relatively steady. In summer, it gathered the cold into itself; in winter, it let its ice extend to us. I had learned that the Gulf Stream current flowed north because the waters there were cold, that it carried warmth from the equator to Norway, that it brought food for the whales.

I had watched the sun creep back from the south in the spring. I knew that the small creatures, moles and weasels and chipmunks and ground squirrels, could live through the winter because snow came before the ground froze deeply and because the snow blanket stayed over them until spring.

But now, the seasons had become confused. Newspapers said the polar bear would die because the ice caps would melt. I feared that the otters would die, too, if winter snows did not encase the north.

The trees near the spring where my son had sailed pitch boats fell upon one another in a tangle and covered the path to that place where water sprang out of the moss. Tent caterpillars ate the early birch and poplar leaves four years in a row.

Mom saved many of our birches by pasting their trunks with a sticky goo that the caterpillars couldn't climb past, though some swung to the trees on threads they spun from the pines in the neighboring lot. We could not save the trees across the road.

We could no longer safely drink water from the lakes. When we canoed, we carried plastic jugs of water with us; when we camped, we filtered and boiled. How were the loons doing, drinking straight from the depths?

Ticks had always bitten us, but in the past, all would be well if we got them off our legs and backs before they changed from engorged black to triple-sized white. Now ticks brought Lyme disease. As children we had trooped eagerly into the woods; now as adults, we doused the kids in spray before they left, and we checked them over inch by inch when they came back to the house.

The moose were dying. Was it because of the heat? People said that their brains were affected by brainworm, so they were wandering onto the roads.

I saw one on a night as I drove near town. It stood in the ditch, swinging its head back and forth. It swung its head, and it bellowed. The car that had hit it sat with a broken windshield farther up, red police lights streaming toward it.

I drove on.

*   *   *

In the early 2000s, three colleagues and I offered listening sessions on campus for students who might be troubled by impending climate distress. About a dozen students gathered with us for each of the circles.

Two older students in neat black suits and closely cut hair sat together during the first. They listened as younger people spoke of fears for the future. Then one of these elders said in quiet English, "The Somali crisis did not start with a war. First came the drought."

"Yes," the other man said. "And the drought was because the climate had changed. The clouds did not come. The rain stopped. The herds of the cattle tribes had no grass. The fodder available to the camel people became less. There was nothing for the goats. The goat people moved onto the camel people's land; the cattle herders brought their animals, too. There was not enough for the camels. How could they share with these others?"

"What would you do?" asked the first man, looking one by one at the non-Somalis in the room. "Let your children starve?"

We sat together in the silence. "So, there was battle," they explained.

I had read in the news that the Somali crisis was a matter of tribal war. These elders added context that altered the story.

A few students stayed on for the next listening circle. Among the new people who joined us was a third Somali elder. He sat quietly until halfway through when one of the students asked him, "The war in Somalia, did it start because of a drought?"

The man furrowed his brow and nodded. "It did," he said. "Many people and animals died."

"What did you do then?"

"As the animals died, some of us men went to the city, to Mogadishu. We thought we would get work. But there was no work. So we went back to the countryside, and we cut down the trees. We knew if we cut down the trees, we would further dry out the land. If there are no trees, the rain does not come, and when some water falls, it cannot soak in. But we cut them down and we made charcoal, and we took it to the city to sell. We made the drought worse, and we fought among ourselves."

"You were trying to keep your family alive," one of my colleagues added sympathetically.

"I was," he said. "I was a leader there. Now I am your student."

* * *

Life moves in circles. Night follows day as dawn follows dark. Winter comes after the fall, and the time of rain between winter and the time of great heat. Childhood is followed by youth, adulthood by age. Old age transitions toward death. Death itself is not an end but a movement into the life of all that the body and memory become.

To break those cycles brings distress. To insist that night not be dark, that winter not be cold, that old age be like youth . . . all of these run counter to nature.

Run against nature long enough and someone somewhere will bash into a wall. Somali people did not bring on that change to their seasons. The carbon that heated up their edge of the Horn of Africa was mostly set free elsewhere.

* * *

Newspapers announced that researchers had identified the cause of the decline in Minnesota moose. There are too many deer. They carry the brainworm that infects the moose. The deer can survive it; moose can't. Warming winters allow more deer to live, but those warmer winters aren't good for moose. It used to be that, in January, weeks of 40 or more degrees below zero would kill the worms and ticks that trouble the moose. Not now. We will lose our moose.

Not only our moose, of course. They and many others who fill the forests with life. Spruce hen, beaver, lightning bugs, bullfrogs, ravens, pine marten, egrets. How many of them will go? How soon?

* * *

When winds no longer bring rain in reliable cycles to a land, humans take desperate action.

Muna, a high school–aged Somali American, sat quietly in her hijab in my writing class. For her introductory essay, she wove together examples of affronts she had suffered—her youngest brother detained at the airport because immigration officials thought her mother was too old to have birthed him; people crossing the street to avoid encountering her; other students ignoring her presence in the lunchroom.

Her later essay about a recent visit back to Mogadishu was more cheerful. She invited readers to walk arm in arm with her and her eighteen-year-old cousin Halivah through the streets, to eat dinner with the extended family, and to eavesdrop on the planning she and Halivah did in their shared bed at night, dreaming together of the day when, finally, Halivah could also come to the United States.

But then Muna stopped attending class. After a week I emailed her and called. No response. Three weeks passed. Reluctantly, I submitted a "last date of attendance" form, initiating the process by which she would be withdrawn from the class.

The next week, suddenly, she was back. When I told her that she had missed so much class that she had been dropped from the roster, she looked up with fear on her face. We arranged to meet later in my office.

"Professor Hanson, could you close the door?" she asked when she arrived. I did.

"I had to go back home for Halivah's funeral," she said. "And then, at the airport, we were detained by a travel ban. We used up a week to get free." Her voice was almost a whisper; she looked at the floor.

"Halivah died?"

Muna looked up. "She bought passage on a smuggler's boat. It sank."

For a moment we simply sat.

"I knew she was desperate to leave Somalia," Muna said. "I didn't know she would try to escape that way." There was a long pause. "I can't sleep, thinking of her in the sea."

She closed her eyes and seemed to stop breathing.

The boat came from—where? Tunisia? And the wave, from where? The wind? Wind meets water. The water does not actually move, I have been told, only rises and falls. But when it crashes, the boat moves, seems to move. Fiercely. Or quietly. And the people?

"You have to breathe, Muna," I said. "For Halivah."

"My aunt wailed so loudly when she first heard that I hid in my room. I was afraid. When I asked my sister, she wouldn't tell me what had happened. Then they told me. I didn't know what to do. My aunt has given up getting the other children here. She has thrown away her green card."

"You don't know what to do. I don't either. What would Halivah want?" I asked.

Muna twisted the edge of her scarf into a narrow band. "Finish school," she said. "She wanted to come here for school."

"If I can get you back into class, will you finish?"

"How?" she asked.

I didn't know. Not for sure. But I made her a list.

"You do this. First, you rest and let yourself cry if crying comes—but maybe only for an hour at a time. All that time, you remember to breathe, okay? For Halivah. Then, at the set times, you pray—you do pray, right? After each time of prayer, you write for this class for fifteen minutes; set a timer and stop when it rings. Then you eat or walk or care for your body in whatever way it needs. Then you talk with someone who loves you. Then you start all over again. Will you do that?"

She said she would try.

I petitioned for her readmittance. She adapted my plan to suit her own rhythm and followed it—stop to grieve, practice regular breathing, pray, write, care for body, talk to a friend. She finished the class.

And now she is gone. I don't know where. But I think she will finish her degree.

When I think of Halivah and the others crossing the sea in boats that are ready to sink, I too must remember to breathe.

Peace to her, to Halivah. Peace to her, to Muna. Peace to Halivah's mother. May we who yet live be at peace. May we breathe in care for those who are gone and also for ourselves.

Stop. Breathe. Settle.

After any shock, the body
holds back from breathing. Sometimes
breathing must be a decision.

Stop. Now breathe.

Settle. Continue to breathe.

Then, let activity come in cycles,
just as the breath comes in rounds:
inhale, pause, exhale, pause, inhale.

Out of love for earthly life forms, join in
their circular patterns—inhale, exhale, sleep
and wake, plant and harvest and eat.

After settling into your breath, take
fifteen minutes to consider how you could
respond to a crisis in your homeland similar
to those these students have faced.

Would you be likely to run, to freeze,
to attack, to turn away?

Then, from the calm of your breath,
encircle your possibly panicked self with
love. What words would you wish to
hear on that difficult day?

Speak those words now, in absentia,
to the desperate children in Somalia,
to the war-torn people of Yemen, to the sick
in a next pandemic, and to yourself.

5

THIRST

Abdul, a partially sighted student from Yemen, spoke of water in his homeland. "When I was young," he said, "my teacher told me that Yemen would run out of water, but when I went home to tell my mother, she turned on the faucet. 'See,' she said, 'there is water. What nonsense they tell you at school!'" Abdul paused. "Then, a couple years later, the government moved out of Sana'a, the capital city where we lived. It moved because the water was gone. It moved, and it did not take us with it."

"What did you do?" Abdul's classmates asked. "How have you lived without water?"

"My mother learned to grow a little food by putting one drop of water on each tiny plant. 'Abdul,' she told me, 'your teacher was right. Now our water is gone.'"

Yemen has lost water because the people have used up their groundwater.

As a sighted person, I wondered: Could Abdul help his mother drip-water each plant?

* * *

I had heard the words *sugar diabetes* in my childhood and knew people who had it. In private, my parents shook their heads and said that a diabetic was someone with an uncontrolled sweet tooth.

My round aunt tickled my back lovingly when she hugged me; she also gave herself shots in the bedroom. "As soon as she got married," my mother whispered, "she started eating ice cream every day."

Fifty years later, I wrote in my journal, *"I feel I have been ill for a long, long time. And yet, I have only a cold. No matter. I will go on working for an alternate way for humans to live because our consumption-driven, human-centered way isn't working."*

Many of my friends shifted uneasily and changed the subject when I spoke about global warming.

"You're making yourself sick," my friend Bonnie said, "talking about the climate all the time. Can't you lighten up? You're making me nervous."

Maybe the warnings were right. Maybe I was killing my beta cells one by one. Maybe my concern for the health of the earth was upsetting the health of my body.

* * *

A dental technician mentioned that she could tell that I chew on my cheeks. I was quite sure that I didn't, but I had to admit that patches inside my mouth were raw.

Getting to work demanded focused concentration. I began to limp. After leaving the light-rail, I would feel dizzy. While waiting for the bus, I would totter. I would put my hand on a signpost to keep myself upright. Unable to stand through two hours of teaching, I would perch on the edge of a stool.

A wart grew large on my hand. A toenail became inflamed. I searched for something to eat that didn't cause cramps. I cut out dairy and soy, then wheat. Dark chocolate leered accusingly at me from the co-op shelf. I turned aside.

Chicken soup? Not even that sat well. I would open the refrigerator door and look hungrily in. I couldn't figure out which foods were making me sick. I shut the door.

I began to plan my travels around access to a bathroom because my bowels were alternately constipated and diarrhetic. One day I rushed away from the train I had been waiting for, desperately looking for a public restroom.

Pain in my hip joint knocked out half my yoga practice. When I found myself looking with envy at my friends as they stretched into a respectable forward bend, I decided to visit my doctor.

She sympathized, gave me a salve for my toe, and described a duct-tape treatment I could try for my wart. She made sure I had an eye exam coming up, scheduled a colonoscopy, and prescribed physical therapy for what she thought must be a labral tear in my hip.

Two weeks later, I arrived at my physical therapy appointment, only to spend the hour in the women's room, doubled over with cramps.

My pee smelled strangely sweet. My bathroom toilet bowl was becoming stained. I acquired what I assumed was a yeast infection.

The extra pounds I had accumulated in my fifties dropped away. My hair stopped getting dirty, even stopped falling out. I never smelled sweaty.

Then, one marvelous day, I noted that I could see my students' faces and could read road signs without glasses. For one glorious month, I could see clearly.

My body was drying out, the eyeballs and membranes dehydrating. Starved for sugar, my body was consuming its own muscles and fat.

* * *

Abdul, the student from Sana'a who told his mother the country would run out of water, became silent, almost sullen, later in the term. We had begun to discuss human population. He could not agree that more than seven billion humans is a problem for the earth.

In 1970, twice as many wild animals shared the land as do today. Now, 97 percent of the mass of land animals is made up of humans and our pets and our livestock; only 3 percent of our moving companions are wild.

As a class, we went over the options. If we keep adding people at a rate similar to the one that has gotten us to the current seven billion—adding them through childbirth and increased life span—we'll need to solve the resulting resource and justice problems in one of three ways:

1. We could colonize another planet. But none of us at this college would likely be chosen to go there. It would be hard to send away four billion extra folks. No water-rich planet lies close enough.
2. We could slightly slow our increase, as some research indicates we are doing already, and all agree to live with the amount of resources actually used by an average Mexican farmer—little electricity, no air travel, no red meat, no imported foods or gadgets.
3. We could significantly decrease the number of humans—either quickly through famine and war or, more pleasantly, by cutting back on reproduction, each set of parents agreeing to have, at most, one child.

People in the class did not like option two. In fact, those who were immigrants had come to the United States to escape from that Mexican-like level of consumption.

Most students felt that we had already chosen the war-and-famine path of option three. More hopefully, about a quarter of the class announced that they had decided, with some grief, to have no children or, at most, one.

We spoke of that final, happier part of option three. If we could get the number of humans back down to three or four billion, our sources told us, we could all share equally at the level of prosperity that most Europeans have now, though not at the level of consumption of the typical resident in the United States.

Abdul waited by the door as class ended.

"Professor Ranae," he said, "I was not happy with class today."

"I could see that, Abdul," I replied. "Do you want to tell me why?"

"I have twenty-four brothers and sisters," he said. "You are telling me we should not be alive."

"Abdul," I said, "I'm one of four children and I have two biological children of my own. Neither you nor I come from a one-child or no-child family. We're talking about this to protect the future, not to blame the past."

He didn't answer.

"How many mothers, Abdul?" I asked. "I hope your mom didn't have all twenty-five kids."

"Six mothers," he said. "My mom had only two."

"Greetings to all of them," I said. "I'm glad they have had each other to help with the chores."

"Thank you," he said. "I will tell them."

We walked quietly awhile.

"But, Professor Ranae," Abdul said to me, "I want to be like my dad."

*   *   *

In Seattle, while I visited my son and his partner, a consuming thirst set in. I drank sparkling water, flat water, wine, tea. I was still thirsty. During the night I would get up every hour to pee and to drink.

Coming out of the bathroom, I noted that I needed a safety pin to secure even my smallest pants around me.

My mouth tasted like iron. I tried drinking milk in case my body was too acidic. No good. A few minutes later I pulled out the grapefruit juice in case I was not acidic enough. Nope. My mouth still tasted like iron.

In the evenings the physical distress would subside as we walked for daily grocery shopping. The year before I'd had no trouble keeping up. This year I asked if we could slow down.

I checked my symptoms online and got one clear answer: diabetes. That had to be wrong because, I assumed, a person had to be prediabetic before she would become diabetic. *Moreover,* I thought indignantly, *I am not a sugar junkie.*

Maybe what my friends had suggested was true. Preoccupation with climate crisis and drought had unhinged my soul. I had worried myself into thirst.

As my son and I drove with the radio on, an announcer said, "This winter the Cascades have only 7 percent the usual snowpack."

I pushed down a panic. *What would the mountain deer drink? How many more trees would die? What about the butterflies and ferns? What of my son and his endless purchases of bottled sparkling water? Would he snap at me in annoyance if I suggested that he get a filter and drink flat water from the tap?*

My thirst grew.

My brother was in Brazil, exploring methods to reclaim industrial water for reuse. Drought had settled over São Paulo. The Brazilian army was guarding the limited freshwater supply so that people would not steal it.

I imagined myself as one of the mothers waiting in line. What would I give to my children if the water pot I got was small? Would I drink first myself?

Stop, I told myself. *Just stop.* Self-talk didn't work. I was thirsty, and I could not shit.

When I get back to Minnesota, I told myself, *my intestines will relax, the constipation will end, and I will be able to eat.*

Longing for Water

Have you ever been without water?

How do you contend with the knowledge
that many humans and other animals long
for water, fight over access to water?

For what do you thirst?

With whom do you speak about water?

What happens to a body, and to a landscape,
as it dries out?

6

LISTEN AND ACCEPT

Karim would fall asleep almost every day in my class.

"Karim," I said to him, "can you get more sleep outside of class? You're not getting the work done."

He looked at me with red-rimmed eyes. "I don't know, Madam. I have three jobs. I try. I sleep after my night job and before this class when I can, but I'm too worried to sleep."

"This class starts at ten. You must get only two hours of sleep! Can you quit the night job?"

"My brothers are counting on me," he said. "There are seventeen of them. I'm the eldest. I'm the only one in the States. My brothers are counting on me."

*   *   *

As a young child, Derartu had lived for several years with her mother's mother in a rural part of what had become Ethiopia.

"My grandma told me about climate change," Dee said to her classmates in my ecofeminism class. "She wasn't educated—not in the way of being able to read. But she listened to the land. She could grow anything, and she loved each tree. Oromo people always love trees.

"My grandma told me and my cousins that she could swim. 'Swim?' we asked her. 'How could you swim?' *We* did not know how to swim. There was no water to swim in! Grandma pointed to the valley and told us that it had been a lake, a big lake with hippopotamuses. But now it was gone; already it was gone in my childhood.

"Grandma didn't know why the climate was changing," Dee said, "but she linked it to the arrival of cars. She said that the earlier foreigners had done bad things, but that none were as bad as the British, who came with tractors and fertilizer and cars. She would have nothing to do with cars.

"The trees were dying, Grandma said, because the rains were not coming like they used to. The cattle could not get food. The new ways of trying to feed them, she said, were killing them instead.

"It's all on that NASA website about climate change," Derartu announced, "all that my grandmother told me.

"When Grandma grew old, she had to move to the city. The land was not fertile anymore. All her children had left the village. She was sad. She grieved for her grandchildren because they would not have the good life she had had."

*　*　*

Alex, an immigrant from northern Russia, raised his hand in my global studies class. "Dr. Hanson," he said, "I've been getting texts from my friends back in Russia. They told me that yesterday great holes opened in the tundra near their houses. Here are pictures— see the gaps in the ground? My friends are afraid. They don't know what's happening, and no one from the government has come to check. They think a hole could swallow up their houses."

Alex was the first to offer personal evidence of the warming that was causing sinkholes to open in the tundra.

*　*　*

When the train from Seattle arrived back in St. Paul, I stumbled to the light-rail station and onto a car. As soon as I sat down, I lay my head on my suitcase. After getting off at my stop, I sat on my bag to await a bus, unable to walk the five blocks home.

I unlocked and entered my house, but I didn't unpack. I made a small nest of blankets and went to sleep.

When I woke, I realized that I would not be able to teach the next day if I couldn't pull myself together. So I called the doctor's office to ask for help with constipation. "Also," I said, "I'm very thirsty and nothing I drink helps." The receptionist wrote down my words and said someone would call me back.

Late in the afternoon, having received no callback, I called again. A nurse told me that there were no openings that day, but that I could see the doctor later in the week. "If you don't want to wait," she said, "you can go to urgent care."

I wouldn't be able to teach the next day without help.

Before leaving home, I opened the freezer door. My daughter had stashed one frozen raspberry treat there. I ate it. Amazingly, it tasted good.

Above the urgent care desk, the wait time sign read "120 minutes." As long as I could sit without moving, time made no difference to me.

Two hours later, a nurse practitioner listened as I explained that I was unable to eat because I was severely constipated.

"I think," she said, "that you have diabetes."

"No," I said. "I've never been prediabetic."

"Is it okay if we check your blood and urine anyway?" she asked.

"Sure," I said. "If you'll help me with the constipation."

Half an hour later she told me that I was, almost certainly, in a diabetic crisis.

"How do you know that?"

"First," she said, "I could smell it; some of us can. And then we got your blood sugar numbers."

She made me promise to go straight to the hospital. "Go now," she said. "Otherwise I'll call an ambulance."

I told her I would go.

"And you won't drive yourself?" she asked. "You have a ride?"

I said I'd call for one.

I texted my med-student son, *"Jos, the nurse practitioner says I have diabetes."*

"Mom, what are your numbers?"

I texted back the numbers I'd just been given, having no idea what they meant: *"BG 346; urine 500."*

He stopped texting and called. "Mom," he said, "you go to the hospital. You've got to see a real doctor. I'm calling for help."

I texted my siblings. *"I'm on the way to the hospital. They say I have diabetes."*

"You?" they responded. I had been the child who willingly ate whole foods and grains, who didn't even like ice cream. But I was the one who got the disease that Mom had warned them about.

At the emergency room, I begged for water, my refillable bottle having run out. The receptionist said she'd have to ask a doctor. *Really?* I thought. *They can refuse a person water?*

After a time, someone offered me a bed.

In a clearheaded moment, I called to leave a message for my dean: "I don't think I can teach my classes tomorrow. Would you do what is needed to cancel them?"

The doctors arrived. They asked questions, ordered an IV. I relaxed with the cool of saline flowing into my vein.

Slowly, my thirst declined.

Someone told me I had a pH of 5 and ketones of greater than 80. "Diabetic ketoacidosis," someone said.

People bustled about. But, over me, a great calm settled. My thirst was subsiding, and I hoped that, soon, I might sleep. I had heard the name of my disease, and, with that, my task felt complete.

Once, when I opened my eyes, a small gnome was sitting on a stool. He twirled on the round seat, his feet not touching the floor.

He looked me in the eyes and said, "I am going to take you out of this."

I thought he meant out of life. I looked away. I did not want to die. I also noticed, with surprise, that I did not want to go home.

Sometime later someone told me that insulin would be added to my drip.

"We'll be sending you to an ICU room in the burn unit because that's the only bed we have."

At 4:00 in the morning, I arrived at intensive care, embarrassed to be wheeled in on a cart. The room had a stone tile floor and thick soundproof walls. At 5:00 a.m. I texted my son, *I'm settled into a pleasant space and hope to sleep.* But with four nurses taking my vitals and a doctor ordering an EKG, sleep seemed a rather far reach.

The Voice of the Body

What, just now, is the
nearest body trying to say?

Yes, that one; the one that is you.

Do you hear it?

Will you be still and listen?

7

RELY ON A DEEP, COOL LAKE

The next day was a blur. Someone said I definitely had diabetes as well as ketoacidosis. I had visitors—my cousin, people from my Quaker meeting. Doctors came and went.

I called in sick for the week.

On March 18, dawn came with clarity. My blood sugar was 77; I could think and, more importantly, I *noticed* that I could think.

A bit later a doctor came in to tell me that my blood sugar was now 86.

"Great," I said. "Let's keep it there. I've been sick all these last weeks, so sick I didn't even know I was sick. I don't want to go back to that."

"I'm glad you feel better, but we need to back off on the insulin," he said. "It isn't good for your body to change sugar levels so quickly. And we haven't yet conquered the acidosis. You now are at 7.18."

The normal pH for a human is 7.4. I was still off by .22.

* * *

73

When the doctor came back later, he said, "We're getting where we need to be, but I must tell you that you are most assuredly diabetic."

"How did that happen?" I asked him. "I was never prediabetic. Isn't a person supposed to get a chance to fix it?"

"We don't know how this happened, and we don't know if you're type 1 or type 2. Do you know the difference?"

"No."

"If you're type 1, your body isn't producing enough, or maybe not any, insulin. If you're type 2, your body isn't able to use the insulin that your pancreas produces."

"Will you be able to figure out which I am?"

"We'll have to wait a few weeks to be sure. We've sent in a blood test to detect any antigens. Antigens stimulate immune responses to activate white blood cells. Their presence in your blood would indicate that the beta cells—the ones that produce insulin—have been attacked and destroyed."

"What did I do to kill my beta cells?"

"You probably didn't do anything," he answered. "With daily insulin injections you should be quite fine, whichever type of diabetes you have."

"Can't you just give me enough insulin now to take care of it?"

"Actually, no, we can't. You'll have to take insulin every day for the rest of your life."

"Shots?"

"Yes. You'll be able to give them to yourself." He paused. "That troubles you?"

"Not the shots," I said, "but I've always planned, should things fall apart, that I'd be able to canoe off into the woods and survive on my own."

*　*　*

Two hours later, the doctor came back. "I have good news for you," he said. "I checked this out. You'll be able to live in the woods for up to three months. If you can find a deep, cool lake and a waterproof container with a rope, you can drop your insulin in that container to the bottom of the lake. Then your insulin will remain usable so you can live by yourself in the woods."

I smiled at him. *All I need to do,* I thought, *is keep my lake cool.*

* * *

I asked a nurse, "They don't know if I'm type 1 or type 2. Which should I be wishing for?"

"Type 2," she said. "That way you'll be able to control it with food."

An hour later, my blood sugar went high. I recognized the feeling—restlessness, foggy head, irritation.

I called the nurse to prick my finger and give me more insulin. The number she read back was 237, far from that comfortable 86.

"We have to wait for doctor's orders before you can have more insulin," the nurse told me. "You're smart. You'll do okay. When you're home, you can control it yourself."

"But he made a mistake. I feel rotten. I need some of that . . . whatever that drug is."

Another nurse said, "You have a lot to learn."

* * *

Someone gave me a pamphlet. I began to read:

Islands in the pancreas called beta cells (or, more picturesquely, Islets of Langerhans) produce insulin. Inside every cell of our bodies, mitochondria wait for sugar. Only the mitochondria know the secret for turning sugar into action. But the gates of the cells remain tightly shut against that glucose until insulin comes coursing through the blood to open them. Once the insulin produces its gate-swinging magic, the mitochondria gobble up the sugar and toss out heat for movement and thought.

Shockingly, the beta cells sometimes succumb to attack. They die. Then, no insulin travels the bloodstream, and nothing opens the cells. Sugar knocks against the walls of the cells, but it cannot get in. Glucose piles up against glucose, pushing en masse against the walls of the cells, clogging the blood. Inside, without glucose for their production line, the mitochondria wait; they do nothing. No energy emerges. The cells shrivel and die; the mitochondria pass away. Blood vessels fill with riotous sugar, sugar with nothing to do but torment the eyes and the heart and the kidneys.

Desperate, the body begins to eat its fat, its leg muscles, anything it can turn into power for breath and for movement.

The tongue dries out, the eyes change form, hair ceases to grow, and sweat glands produce no more sweat.

That is DKA, diabetic ketoacidosis, a condition approaching death.

DKA had been my state when I went to urgent care. *And that's where I'm headed again,* I thought, *if no one will give me more insulin.*

By the time I was done reading, my blood sugar was 243.

A nurse came. "I'm diabetic myself, type 2," she whispered. "Drink water and walk. Walk as much as you can. That will bring the numbers down."

I began to pace, clutching my hospital gown around me. Up the hall and down the hall. Up and down.

*　　*　　*

Blood flows through the body. Ocean circles the lands. Both are awash with nutrients and salts.

If the pH of either is off, life falters. My mouth tasted of iron when I was in DKA. Too much acid. What is the taste in the mouths of whales in an acidified sea?

My body has a small ocean of blood, one that was aided by ICU drip infusions and shots. Insulin brought my body back into balance.

What can bring balance to the sea?

*　　*　　*

I felt hungry. I asked for food.

A nurse told me there were no diabetic trays.

"Diabetic trays?"

"We need to know how many carb units there are in each meal so that we know how much insulin you'll need."

"Enough so that these numbers come down!" I said.

I called my stepdaughter to bring food. Before she could get there, someone brought me a regular tray, one that had come too late for another patient. Mashed potatoes and green beans, roast beef, and apple crisp.

"You'll need a bolus insulin," said the nurse. "I would guess that tray to be about five carb exchanges."

She assumed I knew what those words meant. "You're saying that I can't just eat?" I asked.

A diabetes nurse educator came and sat by my bed. She had a bottle of insulin, a syringe, a container of test strips, a lancing device, a bag of lancing needles, and a blood glucose meter. She showed me how to put the strip in the meter, position the needle on the lancing device, prick my finger with the lance, put blood on the strip, and read the meter. She handed me a small booklet where she wrote how many units I should give myself based on the number that turned up on the meter and on the number of units of carbohydrate I was planning to eat. She demonstrated how to measure the units of insulin.

She showed me a picture of a plate. "See," she said. "You can cover a quarter of the plate with meat or fish. Then you fill half of it with vegetables, but be careful not to use corn or beans or potatoes. The foods that have a lot of carbohydrates can go on the final fourth of the plate. That might be bread or potatoes or rice or corn. You need to measure that portion so you know how much you're eating."

"I don't know what carbohydrates are," I admitted to her.

She handed me another booklet. "This will tell you how many carb exchanges the food you have chosen is equal to. For every person the carb exchanges are the same. But each person has a different amount of insulin they need for each unit of carbohydrate."

"People really figure this out for every meal?" I asked.

"Here's a list with your current insulin corrections," she said. "But these will likely change over time. Your doctor will help you figure them out. For each unit of carbohydrate you plan to eat, you have to give yourself a shot of insulin according to whatever is in this column. You'll find that the amounts you need change according to the time of day, but we'll only be able to indicate the corrections accurately as we discover your body's needs."

The nurse and I figured out the amount of carbohydrate that the tray in front of me was worth and how much insulin the doctor assumed I needed to "cover" those carbs. Then she gave me the shot that she called the bolus.

"In fifteen minutes," she said, "you can eat. Then in two hours we'll take your blood glucose, which we call BG, and see if you need a correction bolus or if you need to eat more carbs. Here is a bottle of glucose tabs," she added. "You eat four of these for each carb exchange you need to add."

"You can't be serious!" I said. "I have to do this every time I eat?"

"Yes," she said. "And you'll also need a shot once a day of long-acting insulin. Do you prefer to give yourself that in the morning or in the evening?"

Then, she gave me a glucagon gun. If ever my numbers went so low that I passed out, I was to have someone open the case, pull out the gun, break open the seal, mix the powder with the liquid, and then shoot the mixture into my leg.

"Got that?"

"I guess so. But who's going to open the case?"

"Someone you live with." A pause. "Do you live alone?"

"Yeah. I live alone."

"Well, then. Maybe a neighbor?"

We let it go at that

* * *

For times when my numbers might go really high, she gave me another tube filled with longer strips. These were to dip in my urine to check if I had ketones in my pee.

"You think you can handle all this? You're scheduled to be discharged this afternoon."

Before I left, the ward staff assured me that I had done no irreversible damage by waiting so long to come to the hospital.

*　　*　　*

I walked out with a bag full of stuff. I'd need a backpack for test strips, blood glucose meter, batteries for the meter, booklet of carb counts, glucagon gun, glucose tabs, food scale, pen needles, lancing device, lancing needles, and sharps disposal case. And a plate divided into fourths.

I had shown up at the emergency room on March 16 and been diagnosed on March 17.

On March 18, I walked out into the sun.

8

FEEL THE GRIEF

I slept through the afternoon. Then I took out a plate and put the food I had chosen on it, carefully measuring the four portions. I consulted my booklet, added up the units of insulin required, and pulled out the pen. It looked like a tiny caulk gun. I got out a needle, pulled back the paper cover, screwed the needle on the pen, and turned the pen to the required number of units. I pulled up my shirt, scrunched up my face, jabbed my belly, pushed the button. Then I pulled out the needle, watched for blood, unscrewed the needle from the pen, and put it with its plastic protector into the sharps container.

I looked at the time. In fifteen minutes, I could eat.

*   *   *

Before I went to bed, I was to test my blood sugar and then give the amount of correction insulin that my instruction booklet advised.

I sat on my bed, ready. I pulled out the bottle of test strips and the meter and the lancing device. I laid them beside me. I was tired, but I had been told I had to test my blood glucose right before going to sleep.

Getting the lance onto the lancing device was not difficult. But I couldn't remember how to cock the plastic machine. I turned it over. I pressed the button. At last I remembered to pull on the end of the thing. It was ready. I put the device to my finger and pressed the button again. Ouch! Blood spurted out.

I put blood on one of the strips and stuck the strip into the meter. The meter sent me a message: *Used test strip. Insert new strip and apply blood.*

It wasn't a used test strip! It was a new one.

I tried again. Same message.

Each test strip cost twenty-five cents. I had just ruined two. The blood on my finger had dried up.

I vaguely remembered that maybe I was supposed to put the strip in the meter and *then* put on the blood.

I tried that.

Strip upside down, I read on the meter. *Remove and reinsert.* How was I supposed to know which side was up?

I did as the small machine instructed. I pulled out the strip and stuck it in the other way.

Again the meter messaged me: *Used test strip. Insert new strip and apply blood.*

I took out another strip. I put it in the meter, right way up.

I put my bloody finger to the strip.

Strip under-filled, said the meter. *Insert new strip and apply blood.*

I tried once more. Wrong again. I had not waited long enough for the meter to be ready for the blood. *Used test strip. Insert new strip and apply blood.*

Five used and useless strips lay on the bed. My head was foggy with tiredness.

I had been given a help line number to call. I was too tired to call.

I was too ashamed to call. Hadn't the nurse shown me how to do this? Was I too stupid to learn?

I remembered my mother saying, "Sometimes you have to quit trying at night. Sometimes the task comes easier in the morning."

Before going to the hospital, I had been producing one small bag of trash each month. Already, just one day into diabetes, my bed was strewn with trashed strips, none of them recyclable.

I dumped the whole lot on the floor and pulled the blankets over my ears.

I was going to sleep. If I died in the night, then I died. If morning came, well, then, maybe this pricking job would be easier.

*   *   *

Life does not unfold smoothly when basic flows and balances are disrupted. If one element of the body falters—if our beta cells die—then other systems fail. Without the beta cells, insulin cannot be produced. Without insulin, the cells cannot open to sugar. Without sugar, the mitochondria cannot create energy. Without energy, the mitochondria and their encircling cells die. Without energy, the brain cannot think clearly, the feet stumble, the body falls, the knees get scraped. Those scrapes do not heal.

So, too, the earth. One thing off course alters the flow of other things. If the ice breaks off, the shore is not where the seals expected. If birds migrate based on the position of the stars, but the flowers bloom based on the heat of the atmosphere, then the birds on their long journeys will not find their necessary food at the places where they are accustomed to landing.

The body tries other ways to create motion and activity. It burns protein from its muscles. That burning creates by-products poisonous to the body—ketones. Ketones cascade toward death.

So, too, the warming of the earth creates excessive water vapor, fogging the air. The melting of the permafrost may release methane. Both water vapor and methane cause further warming.

One danger piles upon another. Soon many systems collapse. If the collapse is extensive enough, the body dies.

* * *

I woke the next morning and went to my tiny yoga room to sit on the floor and focus on the trees over the wooden deck.

I inserted a strip right side up in the meter, lanced my finger, and waited for the *apply blood* message to appear on the meter. I put a drop on the end of the strip, waited seven seconds, and got a reading. I consulted the booklet and figured the correction. Then I got both insulin pens from my bag. I unsealed and screwed on two pen needles, then poked the correction of short-acting insulin into my belly. I took a deep breath and jabbed in the morning dose of the long-acting type. Then I discarded the needles in the sharps box and recorded my actions in my logbook.

Four days later, I was back on campus. Though I could think again, though I was no longer dizzy, I hadn't had much time to contemplate anything other than carb counts, BG numbers, test strips, and insulin pens.

My eyeballs were adjusting to proper hydration, so they had reverted to a haze my glasses were unable to correct. "They'll settle down," a doctor assured me. "Just give them a couple of months."

I couldn't get the carbs and the insulin right. When my head would feel groggy, I'd sometimes remember to test. The BG numbers would have shot up above 180. Above 150 those first months, I'd feel headachy, panicked, and fidgety.

My doctor had told me not to give a correction of insulin unless the numbers were more than 200, but even nearing 200 felt like hell. I complained to a nurse on the help line and was told that my body would eventually adjust to the high numbers so that I wouldn't feel as bad.

Having my body adjust to high numbers didn't sound like a good idea. The consequences of high BG numbers were clearly listed in the information packet: heart attack, kidney failure, loss of fingers and toes, cognitive impairment.

* * *

On Friday night, I decided it was time for more research into what was happening to me. I sat with my computer and put my symptoms into a search bar.

Diabetes showed up, yes, along with all its complications and possible pitfalls. But another disease came up too—pancreatic cancer. Alarmingly, my ongoing symptoms matched that better than they fit with simple diabetes.

Pancreatic cancer? You die quickly, I had heard. I checked—usually in about two months.

I tried to sleep.

No good. Surely my med-student son knew what else my symptoms indicated.

I called him. No answer. I texted, *"Jos, I know this is silly. Still, do I have pancreatic cancer?"*

He didn't respond.

I texted again.

I sat up in my bed. *Grow up. Look at this. Look at the fear directly.*

Is this what that little man on the chair meant? He said he was going to "take me out."

Two months wasn't long. But perhaps they were all I had.

I could be comfortable dying if I knew that life on earth would go on after me. My body could decompose peacefully under a tree, so long as birds flew above it and flowers still grew.

But if the temperature of the planet rises 4 degrees, flowers will not bloom.

I wanted to stay to fight against that temperature rise. But maybe I couldn't.

Half an hour later, Josiah called.

"Mom," he said firmly. "What are you worried about?"

"I checked my symptoms online. They might indicate pancreatic cancer. When will we know if it's that?"

"Listen to me," he said. "You do not have pancreatic cancer."

"That's nice of you to say," I said, "but I don't think you can know."

"The doctors tested for it," he said. "That first night in the hospital, they tested. You do not have cancer."

"Really?" I asked.

"No. You do not," he said again. "They checked. Can you sleep now?"

The world's temperature was going up. My blood glucose had been going up. We'd brought down one set of numbers. Now we had to work on the other set.

I went to sleep.

* * *

A week later I met with an endocrinologist.

"Do you know yet," I asked, "if I'm type 1 or type 2?"

She consulted the online report. "Type 1," she said. "Your labs came back positive for the beta cell antigen."

"And that means?" I asked.

"That means you can't live without insulin and that your need for insulin will increase over time as your remaining beta cells die."

* * *

One-third of the children in the United States today are likely to get diabetes. But that threat is not spread equally among all Americans.

A study published in 2017 in the medical journal *Diabetes Care* found that "the burden of diabetes is not uniformly borne by American society; rather, this disease disproportionately affects certain populations, including African Americans, Latinos, and low-income individuals."

The epidemic of diabetes is most acute for the more than 5.2 million American Indian and Alaska Native people who live in the United States. According to the U.S. Department of Health and

Human Services Office of Minority Health, American Indian and Alaska Native adults are more than twice as likely as white adults to be diagnosed with diabetes. In some communities, more than half of American Indian and Alaska Native adults have type 2 diabetes.

Why? Traditional lifestyles for those communities rely upon identification with the land and its inhabitants and upon hunting and the gathering of local food. Those activities lead naturally to increased walking and bodily movement. As that traditional life becomes harder to maintain, diabetes increases.

There's more. Increasing evidence shows that endocrine-disrupting chemicals may well be precipitating the development of diabetes. Because these chemicals are found in greater concentrations in places where poor people and people of color live, those are the members of our human community who are more likely to get the disease.

Is it okay if the poorer, darker, more marginalized people get sick or die first?

If we are privileged enough to have the resources to speak, ought we not speak up?

*   *   *

My Brazilian sister-in-law found that her legs were too weak to hold her up. She had been experiencing foot drop for two months. Then suddenly she was not able to get out of bed.

She checked the internet and found the diseases that could cause those symptoms. But she didn't tell her husband, who was working on water reclamation in Brazil that week, and they did not tell the rest of us until later in the summer.

Marcia and Jeff were just back from a visit to the neurologist to see if her muscle weakness could be caused by muscular dystrophy. The family had by then risen to the challenge of my type 1 diabetes. We knew we could get Marcia through MD.

"Did he agree that it's muscular dystrophy, Marcia?" I asked.

"No," she said. "It isn't. It's that disease that the ball player had, that ball player and his mother."

"Lou Gehrig's disease," said my brother. "ALS."

Later that day I checked online. Two to five years. No cure.

* * *

At work my colleague, an Ojibwe Norwegian woman who teaches Ojibwe culture and Native American studies, smiled and told me how glad she was that I was back and okay.

"Pat," I said, "I'm having trouble with this. I've become a weight on the system. I get all this medical stuff. I produce bags of trash now. I have good insulin. I have health care. My life got saved. But we have students who don't have any of this."

"You're right," she said. "On the rez, they don't have much. My sons' friends, three boys . . . their mother . . . she told them she had the flu. She stayed in bed, said she'd get better. Didn't have money for insulin. If she had told me, I would have gotten her some. She didn't tell me. Died."

There, standing together by the copy machine, we put an arm around each other.

"She had had a job with health insurance, but she lost it. Got another one without insurance. I went up to that boss at her funeral. Told him he killed her. He could afford the insurance, just didn't want to give it."

"How are her sons?" I asked.

She shook her head back and forth. "You know."

* * *

I briefly explained my new condition to each of my classes. My students would need to know how to react if I passed out while I was with them.

The next day, a student came to my office. "My mom's got it, too," she said.

"Type 1?" I asked.

"I don't know. Diabetes. She has to wake up every two hours to give herself shots in the stomach. She's pretty sick."

"She live here?" I asked.

"Senegal."

"How do you talk to her?"

"On the phone. I wish I could see her, know how she's really doing."

"Every two hours?" I asked. "All night?"

"Yeah."

"She wants you to be here in the U.S.?"

"She does. She wants things to be better for me. But she misses me, too."

"Greet her from me. Tell her you're doing great in my class."

She smiled. "I will. Yes. I will."

*   *   *

My friend Julie came back from a strategy meeting on a reservation in South Dakota. Julie's a white farmer who often works with Indian leaders to promote regenerative agriculture.

"I couldn't sleep one night," she said. "I took a walk, a long walk, all along the land that we were discussing in the meetings. You know what the only modern building, the biggest building, is on that rez?"

"Casino?"

"No. It's the dialysis clinic. Guess what kind of food they sell in the only store?"

"I don't know. Is it government surplus, like lard and flour and sugar?"

"You got it," Julie responded.

*   *   *

"Mom," my son told me, "the research is showing more and more clearly that type 2 diabetes, which you don't have, seems to happen to people who have inherited risks."

Some people are born with a kind of insulin that doesn't fit exactly right into the openings of the cells. The sugar can't squeeze in easily to get burned by the mitochondria.

That was helpful when people spent the days walking, lifting buckets of water, cutting down trees, and carrying children. Constant activity squashed the sugar right into the cells.

During lean months, ones our ancestors called "the starving times," people whose bodies used carbohydrates efficiently that way survived better than their frailer relatives, who used up the sugar soon after it reached their bloodstreams.

Then our lives changed. More people got desk jobs, and their kids were made to sit still through long school days. The wild rice and rye and green beans got replaced with Wonder Bread and Little Debbies.

We have lots of sugar in the blood now and not much demand for muscle exertion. For those with energy-efficient cells, the change to a food-rich, leisured life is no good.

Often, they are blamed for the results. Doctors imply that if they would just control what they eat and go to the gym more often, then their diabetes would be cured.

Even family members look at people with diabetes accusingly. *Can't control yourself,* they think.

But those type 2 diabetic cells are starving, begging for food, because the insulin just doesn't work right, doesn't open them up. It doesn't help if the sugar is cruising around, clogging the blood. If the insulin can't open those cells, the mind fogs over, and the cells plead: *Just a little more doughnut! Just one more lemon drop! I can't keep you thinking with nothing to burn.*

The craving is genetic. The mismatch of the insulin with the cells is inherited.

*   *   *

In 2018, more clarity arrived. The *Lancet Planetary Health* journal reported on a massive study demonstrating, conclusively, that fine particles—primarily from vehicle exhaust—contribute to type 2 diabetes. In fact, in 2016 alone, such pollution was responsible for

3.2 million diagnoses of type 2 diabetes and 8.2 million lost years of healthy life. The burden of these particles, the article announced, falls most heavily on poorer countries and neighborhoods.

*   *   *

There is no way to make the grief easy.

We have to feel what is to be felt.

Despair. Grief. Rage. Guilt. Sometimes a deep aching sorrow that reaches over ethnic borders and across generations.

In 1862, in the Minnesota River Valley, the Dakota were starving. Many German immigrant families had settled on the strip of land that treaties had promised would be saved for the Dakota alone. The money, food, and tools the U.S. government owed the Dakota never reached them.

When the young men told their leader, Little Crow, that they wanted to fight instead of starve, he replied that they could not win a war; the white settlers were too numerous. Yet, he stood with his young men. "You will die like rabbits when the hungry wolves hunt them in the Hard Moon," he said. "I will die with you."

Little Crow did not die with the hundreds who fell in the war of 1862. He was banished with his people to the Dakota Territory. A bounty of twenty dollars was placed on the head of any Dakota who returned to Minnesota. Those folks who killed a person they thought to be Dakota could scalp that person and send the scalp to the state government. In return, they would receive a payment.

As he grew old, Chief Little Crow longed for his homeland. So, with a younger man, he walked back. After the long trek, he was hungry. He reached for raspberries he saw hanging alongside his path.

When a white farmer noticed Indians eating berries that he thought of as his own, he shot at and killed Little Crow.

The farmer received twenty dollars from the government. Then, by sending Little Crow's wrist bones to prove that the man he had killed was the chief, the farmer was given twenty dollars more.

Into my own lifetime, the scalp and wrist bones of that grandfather, Little Crow, were on display at the Minnesota Historical Society.

May we sit with this grief for a time.

Little Crow's bones have now been returned to his people. Some apologies have been made. The farmer is dead. May his family find peace.

The college where I work lies on Dakota land.

I ask those ancestors to stand with us as we move through these sorrows.

Practice for Mourning

What is your practice for living through grief?

- Some make art to honor species
  as they become extinct.

- Some write griefs on small slips of
  paper and bury those slips in the soil.

- Some harvest sweetgrass to burn
  and to smudge.

- Some write each grief into a poem.

- Some weep, arms round their knees
  and rocking to and fro.

- Some lay stones, one for each
  sorrow, in a line upon the ground.

What is your practice for living with grief?

9

CONNECT HUMBLY

How did I get diabetes?

"It might have been a virus," said my endocrinologist.

Because I don't wash my hands enough, I thought.

"Does anyone else in your family have type 1?" she asked, filling in a form for the Centers for Disease Control and Prevention.

"My cousin might," I said, "but I always thought he was type 2. My mom was told she would get diabetes, but she never has. She thought all my siblings would get it, but they didn't. Only me."

"That wouldn't be type 1 she was worried about. Never mind. It isn't usually genetic anyway."

"Does it come from stress?"

"That could contribute. Some think so."

Had I created this? I was costing the medical system thousands. My copay for the hospital stay was $25. Someone else was paying a lot, and it could be my fault.

"Have you considered a pump?" she asked.

Those first months, my blood sugar would go down 100 points if I gave myself one unit of insulin. This was awkward since I felt ill when my blood glucose was 150, but I'd be in real trouble if it went down to 50. Measuring out half a unit was a trick.

The endocrinologist searched out a pediatric pen that had half units. I could use it to come down 50 points. Big improvement.

But a pump, she explained, could dispense insulin in as little as .025 parts of a unit.

"Wouldn't a pump cost even more?"

"Usually it's covered by insurance."

I was having trouble maintaining my energy through an entire class. I couldn't possibly check my blood sugar every fifteen minutes. The continuous glucose monitor, she explained, could come with a pump or even be used without a pump. It would let me know if my numbers were going up or down and would, to a certain degree, tell me what the BG was.

"If your blood sugar fluctuates much, you'll more likely end up with complications," she told me.

Throughout all of human history, save the last twenty or so years—and even today throughout much of the world—getting type 1 at my age would have meant the end of life.

* * *

Two months before my diabetes diagnosis, my cousin Kenny had gotten an infection in his heart, a result of his diabetes. The infection could have caused his death.

He lived five hours away, so I spoke to him on the phone: "Kenny, I love you."

He had gotten a replacement valve and lived.

After my diagnosis, I called him again. "Hey, I'm diabetic now, too. I had no idea that living like this was so hard. How have you done it?"

He laughed, glad for a family companion.

Six months later, his body showed a general infection, and he was flown to the University of Minnesota hospital.

When I visited, I noticed that his fingers were so toughened from years of poking that the nurse couldn't draw blood.

"You got to try near the nail," he told her.

He had lost many of his toes, and his feet were infected; both might have to come off. His heart needed a pacemaker. The infection was spreading.

His blood sugar problem was low on the hospital's priority list.

He couldn't press the call button because his hands were stiffened mitts.

When I fetched a nurse, Kenny said, "I need four units of insulin. I need them now."

"We have to wait for doctor's orders," she replied.

I had never been interested in his illness before. But I asked him there in the hospital how he had first found out that something was wrong. He said that when he was a kid, one day plowing the north forty, he felt so thirsty that he started driving the tractor back to the cream shed after each row to drink a big glass of milk with chocolate syrup in order to be able to keep plowing. That day his sisters decided he had to see a doctor.

From then on, he gave himself shots. "You had to boil needles back then," he said.

"You did it by yourself?" I asked.

"Yeah." He laughed. "The nurse took out a big ole orange and she had me jab the needle in it. Then she sent me home. I did it after that in my belly on my own."

"You were how old?"

"Eleven, I think."

"And you've kept yourself alive for fifty years! How do you do this, Kenny?"

"You've got to want to live," he said.

"And you must have used the insulin and eaten carefully."

"Well . . . I did." He paused. "On the days I had insulin and the right food."

He changed the subject and sang: "'Precious Lord, take my hand, lead me on, help me stand. I am tired, I am weak, I am worn.' Don't you just love those old gospel songs?" he asked me as I stood by his bed. "Can't you just hear my dad and your dad singing them?"

*   *   *

I discovered that nine of us in my paternal grandmother's bloodline are or were type 1.

No one had told me, and no one had told Kenny; no one had thought to. Probably no one put the numbers together.

Maybe there were more.

*   *   *

A TSA employee at the airport told me that I could get over my diabetes by eating only cherries. My mom, still a natural food adherent at ninety-five, agreed; she told me she had known a man who cured his rapid-onset diabetes by hiring on at a cherry field and eating nothing but what he picked.

In my global studies class, when the topic turns to climate change, a few students inevitably announce, "We don't have to worry; the tech people are working on a solution." Other students often answer back, their voices tight with urgency, "Technology has gotten us into this mess; it can't get us out. We've got to start living off the land."

The conflict spreads beyond the classroom. A friend in a meeting on climate solutions slammed a book shut. "I will not," he yelled at the rest of us, "look at anything that considers nuclear power as an option."

We may have to consider everything. One day I might try cherries.

It's all on the table now. First, we have to listen to those with whom we disagree. Then, working with them, we have to create something new. And together, we need to bring back some things that are old.

*   *   *

By 2015, almost everyone knew the climate was in trouble. Many people close to me understood what that could mean. Together we were working to limit the damage. We were building resilience and preparing for coming uncertainties. We became a clan of sorts. Having that community brought me deep, unexpected joy.

On campus, my colleagues and I hosted another listening session. "How are you thinking and feeling about climate disruption?" we asked.

An African American man stood up from the back row. "We have to bring the racial justice and the environmental groups together," he said. "I hear that you in this room get that, but a lot of people don't. Climate and racial justice activists must cooperate. When ecological troubles hit, they slam into my neighborhood first. We need you with us. We need you out on the streets."

"Who is he?" I asked a colleague as we left.

"Kirk Washington. He used to be a student here. He's a poet and a politician, a community leader."

"I want to work with him," I said.

*   *   *

By 2015, I had gained an additional community: the whole hidden guild of diabetics.

Students came to me, some acknowledging their own diagnoses. I had never understood that people lived like this—attending to their bodies twenty-four hours a day, every day of the week, eyeballing food to count out its carbs.

I joined a pump-users' support group where one of the attendees warned me the very first day, "Diabetes is like being pecked to death by a chicken." Everyone around the table laughed.

I was relieved to learn that the pump was not a machine that would be surgically implanted into me. Just the same, I was unnerved that I'd have a hole punched in my belly, a tube stuck through that hole, and a little port buttoned to that hole. I'd have a small hose connecting my belly to a minicomputer.

The first evening with the pump, I wanted to bathe but couldn't figure out how to disengage from it. I prodded and pushed and squinted my eyes. My daughter came to my aid, pressed the two small tabs on each side of the snap on my belly, and pulled the pump line neatly off.

I had become a device with buttons and snaps.

She laughed. "You'll get it, Mom," she said, giving me a quick hug. "You'll do fine."

*   *   *

Coping with hypoglycemia, low blood sugar, was next. The doctor said it would happen.

"What'll it feel like?" I asked my son.

"You'll just feel really shitty and probably shaky," he said. "You'll see."

Two weeks later, in yoga class, I came down from a headstand. Something felt wrong. I walked to a wall and leaned.

"What's up? You okay?" asked my yoga instructor.

"I'm suddenly hot," I said. "But I also seem to be shaking and cold."

"Think you should test your blood sugar?"

"I guess."

By the time I got out the kit and stuck in the strip, I was sweating. By the time I got the reading back, I was drenched. I dutifully downed a fistful of sugar pills. When I got home after class, my numbers were fine again, but my entire torso had broken out in hives.

I filled a tub with warm water and let myself recover.

Clearly, I couldn't do this alone. I called my sister to admit the trouble I was in.

My family and friends divided up the days. Each morning someone would check in with me. I'd text when I was leaving home, when I got to campus, when I left to go home, when I was ready for bed.

Some people with diabetes function with ease. Not me. Without the knowledge that others did this, without my friends and family, I would not have managed.

*   *   *

In my writing class, one student huddled over his desk, breaking free from his nightmares by describing years as a child soldier in a Christian army in Congo.

Across the room, another student wrote with pride about his time in Muslim forces on the other side of the desert. Same war.

Then the day arrived for them to share their essays with the class. I worried. They read. They stood up, surprised. They shook hands. That day they were both Minnesotans, colleagues pushing together toward new careers.

*   *   *

Each year, climate disruption increases the flow of refugees to our college.

Tensions arise. Tensions also release. I was present one day when students took over the class discussion.

It was, they said, time to face the N-word. "Why are some of you allowed to use it without being bashed, but when others of us use it we get pushed? We are as black as you are."

African Americans sat together on one side of the circle; new African immigrants sat across from them. Native, Hispanic, Hmong, Euro sat between the two. "First answer us this," said the African Americans. "Why do you Africans act like you're better than us?"

The response was some time in coming. "For us Ethiopians," one recent immigrant said, "you are the descendants of slaves. We are proud never to have been enslaved."

This was the beginning of connection.

* * *

On another evening, a white woman said, "I tried to talk to my grandparents about this climate mess. They said, 'Never mind. It won't happen during our lives.'"

Shocked, I asked the student, "What about you? Did they notice you right there in front of them?"

"No," she said. "I don't think so. They don't care about me. They like comfort. They don't want to change."

Another woman reached out to touch her.

"My family, too," she said. "We were so close. We talked about everything. But now—when I mention what I'm learning from all of you—about racism, about climate injustice—they shut me up. They walk away or tell me to stop. I don't know how to be with them anymore."

* * *

My son, on a medical rotation, told me of his dismay while he was helping to amputate a gangrenous foot from a diabetic man. He asked the guy on the table, "Might you consider ways to keep your blood sugar down so that you could keep your other foot?"

The person on the table replied, "No. Too hard. Just take off that foot. I'll be fine." He found the technician's solution easier than personal and hourly food control.

Counting carbs isn't easy—ten grams in those two tablespoons of cereal, five in that tablespoon of chia seeds, five in the two tablespoons of blueberries, two in the heap of yogurt, four in the tablespoon of milk, none in the egg, none in the kale, none in the oil, none in the balsamic.

* * *

Through MN350, I learned the practice of deep canvassing. With another volunteer as my partner, we walked house to house, clipboards in hand. We knocked first on a door in a suburb where we do not live. We explained that we weren't asking for money, but were interested in finding out what the person who opened that door thought about energy and the climate.

"Climate change—that's not a problem," the first man said. "The climate is always changing."

We talked on. We asked him what concerned him since climate change did not. "The ocean!" he said. "I was in the navy. My buddies still are. The currents are getting thrown off course. You know that? This is a problem."

His friend, standing behind him, said, "He and I differ. I'm concerned about climate."

By the time my cocanvasser and I moved on, the two men were talking. Perhaps later they discussed the reason for that shifting of the ocean currents, how the warming of the north was changing the flow of the seas.

* * *

I had to become at home in my body. I had to learn about the denizens of my gut, the rhythms of my stomach and bowels.

I needed to move deeper into my flesh, listen for its lows and its highs. I also had to move out of my own pride and biases by reading books by and about diabetics, by going to group meetings, by submitting meal plans to dietitians. The manuals and menus were sometimes too complex for me, but as I stuck with them I found that the limitations were usually mine. The meal plans asked me to check carb counts written on the sides of the boxes the food came in, but I didn't eat food from boxes. My food came from bins at the co-op and from my own stove. My nutritionist adapted her suggestions to my practices. I adapted my inquiries to her knowledge base.

I bought a food scale, downloaded apps. I found that a high BG reading was often foreshadowed by a slight headache in my left temple, that a low announced itself with a touch of hunger, but that the hunger could also mean that I didn't have enough insulin in me.

We all have to become at home in our bodies.

As bodies, we are part of the larger body of earth. We eat of it; give back to it. Breathe with it. We have to come home to our soil.

10

ACCEPT BOTH

Natural systems, left on their own, usually run quite well.

My pancreas functioned admirably for sixty-four years.

So did winter. For several millennia.

When those systems fail, or are destroyed or injured or diseased, and when we resort to controlling them technologically, many things can go wrong.

We have, then, to be steadily attentive.

*   *   *

In the first months, my diabetes upended all I had known. At the start, I searched desperately for a way to avoid the implications of my diagnosis. I'd look at the BG numbers—275 perhaps—and think, *What did I do wrong? Are my toes dying?*

I toted a small refrigerator on a cart up the elevator to my campus office, determined to cache away a stash of insulin and food. I tipped the box side to side, walking it off the cart onto the floor. I slithered my body under the desk to wrap a power strip extension cable behind a file cabinet, then backed out to shove the bulky fridge toward its place. My hands had begun to tremble.

I need carbs, I thought, but soldiered on.

A moment later, drops of hypoglycemic sweat peppered my forehead and back, and my legs begin to waver.

I stopped. Fifteen grams of carb and half an hour later, I was strong enough to position that fridge.

Eventually, I had to acknowledge that my natural response to an impending low was to focus intently on something else. Then the low, when it hit, was even worse.

The moment my blood sugar precipitously drops is the worst time for me to handle the drop well. Highs and lows both muddle the mind. Lows cause a person to act drunk. Highs, over time, atrophy the brain.

I began to rehearse what to do when I was in a near low. The litany is simple enough: *Stop. Find fast carbs. Eat them. Sit or lean or lie. Wait. Test. Eat carbs until in the clear. Then bolus and eat a small meal.*

I have learned to disengage from a meeting I'm chairing, a class I'm teaching, an engagement I'm rushing toward, an intense conversation, a paragraph I am writing, or a wall I am painting. I have had to pull off the freeway, leave children for someone else to tend, eat dessert before the salad course. Hypoglycemia does not wait on my convenience—not even until dinner is ready.

*   *   *

To stop, just to stop, often seems the hardest action to take when we recognize the climate catastrophe.

We are each involved in other tasks—we have exams to study for, jobs to get (or get to), children to raise. Our houses need urgent repair; our bank accounts need strengthening. The health care system must be fixed. Refugees should be protected—or sent away. Plastic has to be kept from the ocean. Pipelines must be laid, or pipelines stopped. More food has to be produced. We have to figure out how to pay for our houses, our vacations, our illnesses.

Our brains tell us that we can think about the climate problem later.

But the climate will not wait.

Climate crisis is like both high blood sugar and low. Like high blood sugar, it's poisoning our air and oceans and forests. Like a hypoglycemic episode, it threatens to lay us out flat.

Like a diabetic crisis, climate trauma numbs our brains. The threat is too big to conceive, so we relegate it to the background. There it sits, unsettling everything, while most of us focus with increasing intensity on whatever task or diversion is at hand.

First, we must stop.

The next essential action is to survey the scene. We can act more effectively when the next crisis comes if we stop to assess the landscape beforehand. We do better if we have a plan, even if it is a plan we later choose to amend.

*   *   *

It was a Thursday, so I texted my brother Greg that I was leaving for work and would be there in about thirty minutes. And then I forgot my books in my office and had to dash back. Then I had to test my blood, and I had to eat a cracker, and I had to get to class on time. And I forgot to tell him I was there. Also, I left my phone in my office.

He called me. He texted. He called our sister and our other brother. He called our friend Bonnie. Then, somehow, he figured out how to call my college. When the office assistant and a security guard arrived at my classroom with the note—"Call your brother Greg"—I realized what I had done.

I raced to my office, got my phone, and called him.

"Good," he said. "You're alive. Now I have to kill you." We laughed.

When you're technologically dependent, you can endanger those you love—along with yourself.

* * *

Technology will be necessary to combat climate change. I use warring language here purposefully.

I uproot one species of grass that another might live. I choose to plant milkweed for monarch butterflies, in hopes they might find the one food they can eat; I ignore the Karner blue, a Minnesota butterfly even more endangered. My heart clutches, but I haven't time to save them all.

We are all in this together now, our human numbers being so many. Few species can escape the effects of our actions. What we do, knowingly or in ignorance, causes some to live and some to die.

Without our technological intervention—now, even the planting of lupine and of milkweed, even the rebuilding of wetlands, requires technology—many species would have been lost already.

So, yes—technology. Maybe we will install enough solar panels. Maybe someone will find another way to keep the bulk of methane safely below ground. Maybe, one day, some government or agency will find a way to bring back the glaciers.

Maybe we will learn to work with nature in more gentle ways. Maybe my friends who are implementing farm-scale restorative agriculture here in the Midwest will succeed in saving this breadbasket for humanity.

No matter what, we should talk to one another—including those we haven't yet met. Attending to only our own houses, our own gardens, won't do.

* * *

I kept on making mistakes:

I forgot to bring an extra canister of test strips on a trip.

I forgot to charge my phone.

I forgot my test kit in a locked room.

I forgot to buy AAA batteries.

I forgot to bring a phone charger.

I forgot to bring glucose tabs.

But not all of the mistakes were mine. My diabetes nurse educator had given me a booklet of foods with the grams of their carbohydrates indicated. I used the list to figure out each of my meals.

In those early months I needed to gain weight, having lost my excess in the prediagnosis days. Needing a bit of cushion, I searched out high-calorie foods. Avocado was one. The booklet listed one-eighth of an avocado as twenty grams of carb. I hesitated to include that in a forty-five-gram meal; nearly half of my carb allowance was more than I wanted to give over to a slender slice of green fruit.

One evening, however, I saved twenty grams of my meal for that one-eighth avocado and then went walking with a neighbor. After six blocks, he turned toward his house, and I headed the further block and a half to mine.

Something was off. Winter had covered stretches of the sidewalks in ice, yet I was suddenly hot. Then an instant later, I was dripping with sweat.

Oh crap! I was going low.

I had to get myself home, but my legs had begun to falter.

I didn't dare hazard the icy sidewalk, but chose instead to walk in the street. Car lights came toward me. I concentrated intently, knowing that if I fell, I would not get up.

At the house, I stripped off my sweat-soaked clothes. I tested. Finding my BG to be nearing 30, I reached for the honey.

I ate it. Just in time.

When I was able, I settled into the comfort of a bath, wondering where I had gone wrong.

I checked online and found that one-eighth of avocado is two grams of carb. Someone had typed an extra zero into that booklet. That zero could have killed.

*   *   *

My student Emia, who had been a guide for tourists in Mongolia before marrying a Minnesota mountaineer, told her ecofeminism classmates, "What they say about the glaciers is true. But back home, I did not understand. For years, when I took visitors to the villages, the glacier was there with water flowing from it for the villagers to drink. But then when we went to the villages before I left, there was no glacier. It was just . . . gone. I told the people, 'Don't worry. It will come back. It has always been here.' Now I understand that it will not return. The glacier is really gone."

Other students asked her, "Where will the village people get water?"

"I don't know," she told us. "I don't know at all."

Emia returned to her classmates with advice. "I am teaching my son," she said. "We never had toilet paper back home. But here, he uses so much. I tell him now, 'When you poo, you can use only one piece. We have got to be careful. It goes into the water.'"

I wanted to tell her that one sheet of toilet paper isn't enough for a small boy of five going poo, but I looked into her earnest face. *This practice is helping her,* I thought. *She can bear the worry about the villagers in Mongolia because she is trying to protect the waters here.*

* * *

During my first two years as an insulin pump user, I was often on the phone with Medtronic reps. When my sensor was wildly off, or when my infusion set kinked, I wanted to scream, "Why do you ask me to use this stuff if it keeps waking me in the night?"

I'd call Medtronic for help and listen to a recorded voice that thanked me for calling and gave me options to press. Then I'd be told (again) that the help line is "available every day of the week, even weekends and holidays." I'd listen, sometimes for an hour, to jazz.

When, finally, someone picked up the line, that person would always follow a script.

"Could you tell me your birth date? And your zip code? What is the email that we have on file? Thank you for verifying your identity."

At last I'd be allowed to explain my problem. "Look, I'm sorry to bother you, but I'm really quite tired and I don't know what to do. My sensor has woken me up three times tonight saying that my blood sugar is low, but each time when I check, I find that the number is fine. Then I go to sleep and, an hour or so later, the sensor beeps again. I'm afraid to turn it off in case I really go low, but I'm becoming crazed. Have you got some advice?"

"Well," the voice on the line would say, "I can see how frustrating that must be. Do you happen to remember what your blood sugar was when this happened?"

"I just told you, it was fine—about 95 or 105 each time."

"Would you tell me where you've inserted the sensor? Did you check to see whether it was inserted through scar tissue? Is it at least two inches from your navel and at least one inch from your infusion site? Do you alternate the sites each time you insert?"

"Yes!" I'd say. "It's not on any scar; I haven't had this disease long enough to get scars. It's not by my belly button, and not under constricting clothing, and not where my body bends a great deal. It's not near the infusion site. But that doesn't leave many places, does it? I'm running out of spots."

Sometimes, I confess, I have yelled. Sometimes the calm voice on the line, giving me good advice that (mostly) I already knew, seemed the height of stupidity.

"I understand how frustrating it is when your pump tells you that you are going low when actually your blood glucose is high, but are you sure you checked correctly? Did you wash your hands before checking?"

"No, I didn't. I was sleeping."

"Might you have calibrated too often today? Did you, perhaps, calibrate when the pump was showing an up arrow, or even two? I see from the online record that you calibrated within half an hour of giving a bolus this morning. Our best advice is that you refrain from calibrating so close to a bolus. And, looking back a bit further, I see that you calibrated twice within a few minutes last night. That can throw the readings off significantly. Could I go over the suggestions about calibration with you?"

"Look," I'd say, "just tell me what to do now. Should I give up on this sensor or try a new one? I'm tired and tomorrow's a busy day. Can't you just make the thing work?"

"Why don't you turn it off and then turn it back on again?" the person would suggest. "That could work."

"Should I tell it that this is a new sensor when I reconnect it, or that it's the same old one?"

"It isn't a new sensor, is it?"

"No, but someone I talked to last week said that starting it as a new sensor if I've messed up the calibrations could give me better readings."

"I can't advise you to do that."

"Okay, okay. I'm turning it off. I'll probably live until morning."

"Before we go, I need to ask you a couple of questions. Is that okay?"

"Sure, I guess," I'd say.

"Has this event resulted in a serious injury or hospitalization?"

"Good lord! You already know that I'm at home, just trying to get some sleep!"

"I apologize, but we're required to ask."

Medtronic was doing quite a bit to keep me alive. Each person on the phone had a job that depended on following that script.

Finally came the day when the rep forgot to ask that last question and I was able to laugh. "Hey," I said. "Last week the rep had to call me back later because he had forgotten to ask if I was in the hospital or seriously injured. So, let's get through that now. I'm at home. I'm annoyed with my pump, but nothing seriously damaging has happened. Okay?"

"Thank you," she said. "I was just about to ask."

* * *

One afternoon, I rushed from campus to get home and make dinner for my mother, who was visiting for a week.

I'd already eaten all the food I had brought for the workday. I got into a nearby Car2Go and began the fifteen-minute drive home. My blood sugar numbers were good.

Then, mid-freeway, the traffic stopped. We sat. The traffic going the opposite direction stopped.

We sat for an hour on the highway. The emergency vehicles that pushed past us indicated that there must have been a major accident. I realized that someone may have died.

I checked my blood sugar. It was falling. I checked again. It was falling fast.

An insulin pump can bring the blood sugar down by adding insulin to the body, but it can't take insulin out in order to make the blood sugar go up. Only sugar or other fast carbs can stop a blood sugar drop.

I searched my bag for sugar. Nothing. I dug through my pockets. No food. I looked again. I had nothing at all to eat to raise my numbers.

If I were to pass out from a serious low blood sugar, and if my foot were to fall against the gas pedal, my car could plow into someone else's car.

I called my sister Heidi.

"The traffic on this freeway has been stopped for an hour, and I'm blocked up against the median by other cars," I told her. "My blood sugar is going low. I have nothing to eat. I've searched the car. I've thought of knocking on a neighboring car window and asking for sugar, but then I'd have to get out of the car."

She considered. "No," she said. "I think you should call 911."

"The police are all up ahead, but, yes, they could make their way back to me." I took a long breath. "If my blood sugar keeps going down, and I can't get out of here, I'll pull as close as I can to the barrier, turn off the car, and call."

Just then, our line of cars was instructed to move ahead and pass through a break in the median before turning back to drive the wrong way on the other side of the freeway.

 I got home just as the sweating began.

* * *

The next day in my first class, I was still shaken. "I was stuck on the freeway after that horrible accident," I said.

"You know who it was that died," one of the students said, her face a mask of pain. "Kirk Washington. We lost Kirk last night."

Kirk had been driving east when a car going west jumped the median and hit him head-on. Someone else's life conditions had sent her car out of control, across the median, and into the path of Kirk Washington's car.

I had never told Kirk that I wanted to work with him.

* * *

At the end of May 2017, I returned with my close family to Seattle for my son's graduation from medical school.

We were there to celebrate. Except that my sister Marcia was near death.

On May 26, my son walked across the stage and accepted an MD diploma. Two minutes later I received a text that Marcia had entered her final deep sleep.

That night, after a glorious party for my son, after a day of anguish with my sister and her family, I heard something near me beginning to moan. The sound grew more insistent when I lay down.

Throwing back the covers, I discovered the whine coming from my insulin pump.

I looked closely. The pump had frozen. It was neither delivering insulin nor able to respond to a persistent pressing of keys.

I turned the pump off and then back on. It functioned for half a minute and started to howl. I turned it off, took out the battery, installed a new battery, turned it on. It functioned for another half minute and then froze.

I called out for my daughter, who came and sat by me. "Mom, I'm here," she said. "Do whatever you have to do. I'll stay with you."

I called Medtronic. The adviser told me to turn off the pump for two hours, use my backup insulin delivery methods, start the pump in two hours, and call back with the results.

I didn't know how much insulin to give myself. Because my pump was dead, I had no record of how much active insulin I was running. I couldn't remember when I had last bolused or how much.

I did my best. In two hours I tried the pump again. Dead.

I called the Medtronic agent. He told me the pump was done for. Because this was the start of the Memorial Day weekend, I would not get a new pump for three days, or maybe for four.

That night I was awake through the dark and into the early break of day.

*   *   *

Two days later, my replacement pump arrived with a booklet of instructions.

When I had first gotten my pump, a diabetes nurse educator had set it up while I watched. Now I was in Seattle—and my sister was dead, and my daughter had just flown away. I was about to go home alone. My emotions were a jumble.

The instruction booklet told me to copy the settings from my old pump onto a page with eighty-nine blank spaces and nineteen check boxes. But my broken-down pump had wiped its settings clean.

I called the help line. The consultant repeated the instruction to copy the settings from my old pump. I told her that my pump no longer had any settings. "Then copy the settings from the online backup," she said. I told her that I didn't have a computer with me that had my passwords and that I didn't know how to get into those settings. I asked her if she could please find them. She couldn't.

We rang off.

Before leaving home, I had written the most critical settings on a card to carry with me, so I programmed those into the pump. Then I did the best I could with the remaining check boxes and lines.

I did pretty well. I got all 108 official settings correct—or close enough to cause no trouble.

However, there was one setting for which there was no line in the booklet. I got that one wrong.

* * *

Oanh, a student from Vietnam, told our class about her family's farm back home, where they raise freshwater fish. Now, in the rainy season, ocean water invades, dumping salt into their ponds.

"Should we switch to ocean fish?" she asked. "We don't know how to raise them; no one wants to eat them. Also, what about our neighbor's rice? They can't raise rice in saltwater."

In the lowlands of Bangladesh salt-resistant rice is being developed. I wanted to tell Oanh about this rice. I wanted to hear whether her neighbors could try planting that rice.

* * *

My first serious low on the new pump came on the way to the Seattle airport. Grief, I decided, was the cause. I quickly ate all the food I had with me. It was just enough to catch the blood sugar fall.

The next low, three days later, was much worse. Thinking I must have programmed the pump incorrectly, I asked both a Medtronic rep and my endocrinology nurse to check over my settings for problems. Neither found anything amiss.

Four days later I went on a late walk with my neighbor Jerry. When I returned home, I remembered that I needed to change both the infusion set and the continuous glucose monitor. I had eaten carefully and bolused appropriately, so I was quite sure that going to sleep would be safe. The monitor would beep to wake me in two hours for a blood glucose check and calibration. After that, it would warn me of any lows.

One hour later I woke, my heart pounding. The sheets clung damply to me. I was shaking. I checked the BG—in the thirties. I ate all the glucose tabs by the side of my bed. Still trembling and dripping with sweat, I made my way to the kitchen to find more sugar.

On the way back upstairs, my legs wobbled. Eating sugar tabs as quickly as I could, I reached the bathroom and crumpled on the floor. I longed for a bath, but realized I might not live to have it.

The shaking did not stop. I tested once more and found my numbers to be in the twenties. I stripped off my wet clothing, still chewing the orange-flavored tabs. Were the numbers going to come up? I needed to test my blood sugar again—*it had to be correcting!*—but the test strip bottle slid from my hands. I pawed over the floor. I couldn't find it. I felt under the tub. It wasn't there.

I knew I couldn't get to the bedroom to reach the top shelf where the extra canisters of strips were, but I still had my phone at hand. I called Jerry and asked him to come. Earlier that same day I had hidden an extra key in the entry. He would be able to get in.

By the time he arrived, I had managed to wrap myself in a towel. He rummaged in my closet for the new box of strips and brought it to me. I tested. Waited. Tested again. The second test said the numbers were headed toward safety.

* * *

When I saw my endocrinologist, she and I set the pump for higher blood glucose limits and talked about precautions. Never again that summer did I change my CGM before going to sleep.

The lows persisted, but during the daytime I could grab my emergency food and sit very quietly until I would catch the drop. I'd stay awake late, eating sugar, until I was sure I would survive the night.

And then, in mid-August, that replacement pump neglected

to record one time that I had changed the infusion set. I called Medtronic to report the discrepancy.

The agent on the line was mystified. She told me that I must not have not changed the infusion set. I had. Then she suspected that I had changed the set but not filled the cannula, the short plastic port that delivers insulin into my body. She was polite, like most help line people; however, she was pretty sure that I, not the machine, had messed up. I told her I had filled the cannula.

She opened the fill-cannula records online.

"Why," she asked, "are you filling the cannula with seven units?"

"Because the cannula I use is a Silhouette," I told her. "When I used to use a Quick Set, the number was 3. Months ago, when I changed to a Silhouette, I was told to change from a 3 to a 7. So, in Seattle when I had to set up my new pump, I programmed the *fill-cannula* to 7."

"The Silhouette," she told me, "uses 0.7. Yours is set for 7.0."

I took that in. After a long pause, I responded, "It should be 0.7?"

I had been proud to remember the 7. Nothing in the setup book-let mentioned the number for filling the cannula. I had remembered the 7, and I had gotten the other options correctly programmed. But I had missed a decimal point.

Each time I had changed my infusion set—every three to four days—I had been getting 6.3 extra units of insulin, units that I didn't know I was getting, units that I didn't need, and units that the pump didn't tell me were active.

* * *

Maybe, just maybe, we'll find some tech response to our climate distress. But it isn't likely to function smoothly.

Tech has saved my life, for now. But tech alone won't cure our climate ills.

For millennia, rivers and forests did fine without human control. But once they are thrown onto the mercy of human technology, humans must keep them constantly in mind.

We can welcome technological solutions. But with caution. The waters will continue to rise.

*   *   *

I corrected the setting. The agent said that she would have a replacement pump sent.

As I set up the third pump, my brother, an engineer, sat next to me. Because the second pump wasn't completely broken, we could copy the 108 settings.

"This is extremely complicated," Jeff said as we worked.

We got to the end.

"There isn't even a line here about the *fill-cannula* setting," he said. "How could anyone know what it was?"

Still, I should have. Once you become part machine, you have to be constantly alert.

How to Die

Marcia, my sister-in-law, accepted some technology that extended her life; then she drew a line. She refused a tracheotomy. With it, she could have lived longer, but without a voice. Already she had lost the use of her hands and her legs. She chose.

Assessing the options, Marcia selected her path toward death.

Assessing her own different options, my student's cousin, Halivah, chose a smuggler's boat. When it sank, she went down.

Let us bow in respect to these choices— and to the decisions yet to be made, yours and mine among them.

II

BEAR WITNESS

When Frederick Banting and his assistant were searching for a way to isolate insulin and to prove that it would reverse diabetes, Banting lived with daily despair. He was causing scores of dogs to become diabetic and then trying to cure them. The dogs died one after another during the surgeries he performed, or because the insulin he gave them did not work, or because he couldn't figure out how to correctly give that insulin. His medical career had failed. His girlfriend, Edith, had grown tired of waiting for him. She wrote to him on March 17, 1922, to break off their relationship. His lab space was dirty, smelly, and inadequate. He was desperately broke, but still managed to drink himself to sleep every night. Meanwhile, all over the world, thousands of children and adults were passing away from diabetes.

Nevertheless, he succeeded. Soon after the sacrificial death of his beloved dog Marjorie, Banting convinced his research team that insulin could keep people with diabetes alive. Not much later, insulin isolated from animal beta cells stopped the dying process in a thirteen-year-old child named Leonard Thompson. Leonard lived another fourteen years until he died, not from diabetes, but of pneumonia. He was the first to survive.

Dan Hurley, a historian of the discovery of insulin, wrote, "What Banting had going for him was desperation."

Desperation is what many of us feel now.

* * *

Martina, a young student from a village in central Mexico, and Amina, an elder student from rural Somalia by way of refugee camps in Kenya, offered to speak to my Quaker meeting. They had not shared their stories before.

"Our trouble began with a drought," Amina told us.

"Ours, too," Martina said. "The rains did not come."

They looked at one another. "Also in your part of the world?"

Quickly the stories tumbled out. "When hunger and fighting came, the men left."

"Our men, too."

"And we had to leave, we women and children. We had to go where we could."

"I also. I hired a coyote—oh, I am legal now! I am legal, but my uncle is not. And, at first, I hired a coyote."

"Children died. Women died. Giving birth as we walked."

"My aunt also."

"To make fires for cooking, we cut down the trees that were left. We knew that this was wrong."

"So many trees—my grandfather, too. He cuts the trees. He sells wood in the village."

As we left the meeting, the women hugged one another. Then they turned to me. "These people were nice," they said. "They listen. It seems like they care."

Please join me in witnessing. Do not turn away.

* * *

Native American ethics tell us that we are all one family. We are family with our winged brothers, the mosquitoes and eagles and doves. We are cousins to the standing folk, the mountains and the trees and the stones. We are sisters to the people with fins, the pike and sharks and carp. We are relatives of the flowing folk—North Wind and Mississippi and Gulf Stream.

We are all indigenous to this earth, though many of us not to the places where we now live. Our ancestors, somewhere in the past, knew themselves to be one with the land on which they rested. Many of us have forgotten what once was known.

We can relearn from those who are indigenous to the lands where we happen to live now.

Although many of us have lost our indigenous roots, each of us can become newly attuned to the place where we reside.

My beta cells are gone. So I sing for them: "Beloved beta cells. Now that you are gone, I know to have adored you. Grateful now, I sing your praise—you magnificent cells that gave me sixty-four years. You weighed my food without a scale, without eyes of your own. You separated carbohydrate from fat, took the measure, timed the moment of entry of sugar into my blood, produced insulin so that the mitochondria might eat. Dear departed beta cells, how I love you now that you are gone!"

*   *   *

A type 1 friend must get her test strips through Medicare. For months, she was allowed only two strips a day. Two strips! I use, on average, seven. How could she test before each meal? How could she test before sleep? How could she possibly protect her feet and her heart with only two strips a day?

A friend of a former student sent this cry: "I just spent $807.96 on insulin, the one thing that keeps me alive. These three vials last me thirty days. So in one month I'll have to go back and get another round of insulin . . . at the same price. I'll have to keep doing so until

I reach my max out of pocket, which is $7,000. Keep in mind I do have health insurance."

In 2017, a twenty-six-year-old man, the son of a colleague, decided he could not afford his insulin. He had been type 1 for only two years. At twenty-six, he was no longer able to remain on his parents' insurance. He had a job but no insurance coverage for the insulin. "We had been worried about the lows," his mother told me. "The highs were what got him." In June, he died of diabetic ketoacidosis.

*   *   *

Insulin, test strips, glucose monitors, infusion sets—all are in limited supply. I draw from that supply and, so far, pay $25 max for my one vial per month. I am doing my best to stay at one vial per month. I can remain with the one small vial only because I have test strips, infusion sets, and a monitor.

Take what you need, Native American ethics teach us. *But only what you need. Leave the rest. Do not take what you merely think might be nice or what you hanker for. Not more than enough.*

Listening to my body is the way I can know what I need.

I can give back. We all can give back. When we take, we are honor bound to give.

If you are in a position like mine, consider sharing. Sharing insulin or test strips or infusion sets is not legal in the United States (though, just the same, it is sometimes done). Instead, we can donate internationally through Insulin for Life.

There is an urgent need for insulin supplies to aid victims of the latest hurricane. As climate change causes more hurricanes, more people with diabetes will need help.

*   *   *

When Martina came to speak at my Quaker meeting, she told us of a decision she had made. Her grandfather, back home in her village in Mexico, persistently asked her to send him money He wanted to buy explosives so he could break up the rock on the mountainside. He thought he could sell stone to the people in town.

"But that rock," she said, "is around our only spring." Wangari Maathai had written, and Martina had read, about how the springs in Kenya disappeared once the fig trees that directed their waters were cut down. When the trees went, the tadpoles went, and the little frogs too, and the plants by the shore, and then the people.

Martina told her grandfather that, no, she would not send money for that. She would help him find another way here.

*   *   *

I needed to understand how this disease happened to me and what I could do to keep it from my kids. So I read Dan Hurley's *Diabetes Rising: How a Rare Disease Became a Modern Pandemic, and What to Do about It.*

First I learned that one out of three American kids will become diabetic. That seemed like an exaggeration, so I checked online. Yes. The American Diabetes Association says that over a quarter of Americans sixty-five and older already have diabetes. It appears quite likely, then, that one-third of the children will get it as they age.

I read the chapter subtitles:

- Does Baby Formula in the First Months of Life Set off an Immune Attack?

- The Risks of Persistent Organic Pollutants

- How Too Little Sun, and Too Little Vitamin D, Might Raise Diabetes Risk

- The Icky Benefits of Dirt, Germs, and Worms

I found no chapter on stress and none on a virus—two ostensible causes of the disease that were mentioned to me when I was diagnosed.

Diabetes was first considered to be of two sorts, one called "juvenile onset" and the other called "adult onset." Then, as adults like me showed up with the juvenile type, the names changed to "type 1" and "type 2," or to "insulin-dependent" and "non-insulin-dependent."

Both types are related to weight gain. But I read that weight may not be the actual culprit. It could be that the kind of fat cells in people is the cause of their diabetes. Some fat cells have immune dysfunction; others don't.

I sat up in my chair when I read this: "Three papers published simultaneously in the prominent journal *Nature Medicine* in July 2009 reported, for the first time, that immune dysfunction in fat cells of overweight people and mice might be the real cause of their diabetes, rather than the fat cells per se."

So, okay—note to my kids: *Be sure to have the right kind of fat cells.*

Note to self: *Get the culture to have easily available, tasty, carblight food. Get it to encourage bodily activity. Get it to back off on blame. This is not primarily an individual's fault.*

Hurley presents evidence that giving babies anything other than human breast milk ("any foreign protein," he calls it) during the first six months of life can set up an autoimmune reaction that could lead to type 1 diabetes, as well as to other autoimmune diseases. In fact, Hurley believes that protecting babies from foods other than breast milk during those first six months could prevent half or more of cases of type 1.

My mom was determined to nurse all her children. I came first. The delivering doctor, just as determined to give me the best possible start in life, whisked me away from her and shoved a bottle of formula into my mouth even before my mother woke from the sleep he had forced upon her.

Mom's willpower succeeded at the births of my siblings; they all got colostrum and immune-supportive early milk. Not me. I, who have always remained the thinnest of the four, got started on formula, and I'm the only one of the siblings with diabetes.

I read on. The third probable cause is what Hurley calls "persistent organic pollutants" (POPs). I looked them up online. Right! They are exactly those chemicals that probably cause the high rates of diabetes in Native Americans, African Americans, Hispanics, and lower-income people worldwide.

What can you and I do? Speak against environmental injustice. Drink water to give our bodies the chance to flush pollutants out. Eat low on the food chain because POPs collect in animal fat. Grow our own food. Buy what is local and in season because that will likely be less exposed to chemicals. Learn about and practice restorative agriculture. Share any privileges we have.

We can also make sure to get enough vitamin D. We need sunshine, lots of it, and we need vitamin D to make up for any sun we don't get. In fact, Hurley's research led him to recommend 2,000 international units of vitamin D_3 a day, especially for children.

Hurley's fourth probable cause is too much cleanliness. That's right. While getting rid of nasty bacteria has prevented many illnesses, becoming too pristine seems to be causing susceptibility to autoimmune diseases.

So, when out in the sun, dig into the soil. Plant. Make compost. Become part of the land where you live.

Hurley's chapter on cleanliness ends with a quote from Joel Weinstock, MD, director of gastroenterology and hepatology at Tufts Medical Center in Boston: "Do I believe that living in a less hygienic environment could be protective? The answer is yes. . . . Children raised on a farm, with large animals, are less likely to get these autoimmune diseases. . . . I tell parents of children with immunologic diseases, let your children play in the dirt, have a dog and a cat and don't wash it, let them be exposed to things around them. It's okay to go to a farm and play near the manure. Just common exposures may be helpful, and probably won't be hurtful. Nobody gets sick from playing in the dirt."

*   *   *

In my global studies class, students began to discuss the Nile. All were Minnesotans, but they came from the Congo, from Kenya, from Egypt, from Somalia, from Ethiopia. Some came from more than one country by way of relatives and refugee camps. They were all able to discuss Nile water politics.

There's a new dam going in somewhere that will take water from somewhere else, and the water is needed by the grandparents of someone in another place, and the dam will likely flood the farms of someone else, and surely there will be a war.

Water truly is life. Or death. Two young Somali women threw pictures up on the screen—skeletal cattle, dry bones, soil cracked open. This was their land without water, they said. This was why they had to plant trees, but—"See those tiny ones? People are cutting down even those tiny trees because they need fuel for cooking their flatbread."

"Yes," someone else said, "they ought to have solar cookers. Where can people get those?"

"Doesn't taste good, Somali bread cooked in those solar things," said a guy.

"You see," said a woman in the back. "You men are the problem. You make us cook the way you like instead of the way that is good for the future."

*   *   *

Moti, an Oromo student, presented the problem of land grab as his research for an online writing class. He hardly had time for the class because he was so involved in trying to find a way to save the fields of his family back home. Ethiopia, he told us, was claiming the farms of the Oromo people, and then selling the land to investors from India or China, who would plant crops behind fences and take the produce across the sea. The Oromo people had nowhere left to put their seeds or to pasture their livestock.

When I asked students in the class if they would like to present their research findings at the upcoming Transition US National Gathering in St. Paul, Moti wrote that he wanted to come.

The evening before his presentation, Moti made use of his guest pass to view the film *Demain* (Tomorrow). Watching, he learned of permaculture and saw farmers planting crops on four levels in tiny spaces. He saw how little water they were using.

The next day he brought his passion for the Oromo land to the conference.

"Permaculture," a listener said. "We have to all learn permaculture design."

Come to Know

Commit to one restraint. Perhaps:

Hang your laundry to dry.

Give up air flight.

Stop eating cows.

Walk when you could drive.

Learn to cook.

Listen with a welcoming face so
you come to know your neighbors—

Those who are differently abled,

And differently clothed,

And differently aged,

And differently cultured.

After you have made your commitment,
record each day how you do. Notice
your patterns for keeping or dropping your
commitment. After a week, recycle the paper.

Then, get to know a tree. Over time. Personally.

12

WALK WITH AND NOURISH OTHERS

For many semesters, I gave students in my ecofeminism classes an assignment that required them to walk in nature and turn their attention to living beings and the land. At first, they were surprised. This assignment did not seem like college to them. But by the end of the semester, most of them reported that they had learned more from these attentions than from anything else they had done that term in any class.

I don't take credit for what they learned. Life itself did the teaching. Here is the assignment they followed:

To explore your own environment and life, you'll spend time each week attending to aspects of the world around.

You will select an ecosystem near you, one that is as natural as you can find. You will visit and learn about that ecosystem, primarily through direct contact by walking and sitting and listening to it, most of the time alone and without cell phones or headsets or other distractions.

In that ecosystem, you will select one tree to attend to in particular.

You will also choose a being at the beginning of its life, one that could benefit from some attention from you. This may be a human child under two years of age or another animal child that is not yet full grown; it could also be a plant that you select and care for.

Finally, you will select someone who is much older than you or who is, for some other reason, closer to death than you are. You will spend time with this person, getting to know her or him. You may or may not talk directly about the span of life and its ending with this person, but you, on your own, will consider the length of life and its beginnings and endings.

Each week you will need to spend two hours exploring or attending to these four disciplines and writing what you discover and learn. Keep a journal where you record what you did during your attending time, what you observed, and what you thought or felt about your observations.

* * *

Callia, who biked daily past a park, was not sure she had time for this practice. But she needed the credits.

She chose one oak from the many that she biked past. She stopped each week to sit with the tree. She expected her visits to bore her.

Quite soon, she was telling others, "A tree isn't scenery. My tree is an individual. I bet every tree is like that. Nothing along the path is just part of the scene. Everything is its own self. You should do this, too; you should come to know a tree."

Now, anytime Callia bikes, she stops somewhere to greet a tree. The world for her has become rich with standing companions.

To know a tree, you have to walk. You have to stop. You need to put your hands on its bark and look up into its boughs.

* * *

Adam Brown's book *Bright Spots and Landmines: The Diabetes Guide I Wish Someone Had Handed Me* has served as a messenger of sanity for me. This young type 1 man said directly that I can't eat whatever and however much I want, not if I want to feel good.

Instead, he told me, I'd have a better life as a diabetic if I'd do six things:

1. Limit each meal to 30 or fewer grams of carbohydrate.
2. Eat almost no refined carbs.
3. Take at least 10,000 steps each day.
4. Find support from my family and friends.
5. Get enough sleep.
6. Keep records.

Brown was right.

He didn't say that doing those six things all the time would be easy—only that I really ought to do them.

Most people I know eat meals with more than thirty grams of carbs. Maybe Brown truly manages never to eat more, but I don't. When I eat with other people, I usually end up eating significantly more. That goes somewhat okay—if I also walk. Even eating thirty grams doesn't work well unless I walk each day.

If I walk to work instead of busing or driving, and walk to the store, and carry my laundry outside to dry, and get up every half hour to drink another glass of water, and walk upstairs instead of taking the elevator, and walk up and down the halls while waiting for a doctor appointment, and walk around the block when waiting for a meeting—if I adopt a practice of walking every chance I get, then taking ten thousand steps isn't an add-on. It becomes a part of the day.

And most of the time it decreases the burden I put on the atmosphere. The more I walk, the less I drive.

*   *   *

One day as I was walking, I heard owls hoot, watched quail court, enjoyed a blackbird orchestra, smelled cypress trees, cooled off in cypress shade, trod on cypress fruit. The people in the cars who moved past me experienced none of those delights. By walking, I also brought down my blood sugar and used no fossil fuel.

Not that walking is always easy. In winter, our sidewalks are icy and the air is cold. Walking in winter, I sometimes miss the hawk overhead because my eyes are focused downward to detect any glint of slick ice.

Even in winter, though, we can find ways to walk. I drag a stretch of yarn with a noisy cardboard square attached down the stairs, around the dining room table three times, into the kitchen, back around the table, up the stairs again, and into each of my rooms. My cat crouches at the top of the stairs, then pounces, races ahead of me, crouches again, catches the cardboard.

Adam Brown made another important point. Most of us won't do today what will pay dividends in twenty years. He tells us diabetics to walk because we will feel better *today*—and also because our families and friends, and cats, will be happier, feel safer, and be more at ease if we take this care of ourselves.

I met an Ethiopian father who has three kids—two of them type 1. He told me, "Type 1 people take care of themselves—eat healthier and get more exercise. That makes them live longer on average than people without diabetes."

* * *

Making the necessary changes in our lives will be difficult. At first they will feel like deprivation and serious loss.

But, as in the early days of COVID-19, we may find that some of our apparent losses actually bring us greater life. Over time, we can adapt.

Just before insulin was developed, Elizabeth Hughes, a teenage girl with type 1 diabetes, lived for three years by following a starvation diet.

This was her meal plan during those three years. On the days when she ate at all, she ate two eggs, one egg white, two and a quarter heaping tablespoons of thrice-boiled string beans, one tablespoon of cream and coffee, half of a small orange, two and a half heaping tablespoons of cod, two heaping tablespoons of thrice-boiled Brussels sprouts, five small olives, a pat of butter, two cups of tea, and two heaping tablespoons of thrice-boiled spinach. On the seventh day of the week, she ate nothing at all. And on the two days before that fast day, she ate half her usual carbs.

If she could accept severe restrictions in order to stay alive, so can we.

We don't have to cut back as far as Elizabeth did. Yet, we *do* have to cut down on purchases of stuff, on travel that uses carbon-based fuel, on plastic, on red meat, and on all that harms ongoing life.

When the restraints seem too much, think of Elizabeth.

Elizabeth stuck to her diet cheerfully as others feasted around her.

She lived to be seventy-three.

*   *   *

At first, when I saw plastic in the roadside gutters, I muttered angrily about people being slobs, fuming that they didn't care about turtles and fish. Then I realized that I could carry a bag as I walked and pick up that trash.

Now each piece of plastic I retrieve becomes a song of love to the sea and its creatures: *"This plastic straw will not choke you. This bag won't stifle your breath. This bubble wrap won't catch on your shell."* In the nights when I wonder if I have done any good that day, I celebrate that gathered-up trash.

*   *   *

"Nearly everything," Winona LaDuke told our college community, "is considered alive by Native peoples."

Soil is alive, as full of life as we are. Rocks are alive—in them is all the nourishment that bacteria need. Winds are alive—brushing the trees, rustling the grass, speaking to us.

Even the dead can live again in our memories. As I walk I hear my deceased father whistle through his teeth, "Ranae! Do you see that white-legged bird?"

WALK WITH AND NOURISH OTHERS

We can come to know other forms of life, across species, even across time.

Try it. As you walk, talk to the trees. Learn the names of plants, or give them names yourself. It's harder to ignore a being once you can speak its name.

Talk to birds. Thank them for their songs.

Bend gently to pat the soil.

Use your energy to nourish others as well as yourself. But, first, learn who those others are and ask them what they need. When we force the aid we think is right onto others, we violate them.

13

WATER, PLANT, AND MAKE SOIL

Omar, a Somali American immigrant, announced to the class that, although he knew the names of forty types of trees back in Somalia, he didn't know the name of even one species here. He started to learn about his new home by sitting with an elm.

Ali, another Somali American, settled into one patch of land on the bank of the Mississippi during the semester. When summer came, he returned to Somalia to learn from his mother how to plant and water mango trees.

Group after group of Somali students, inspired by reading Kenyan activist Wangari Maathai, and by memories of their own grandmothers and grandfathers and uncles and aunts, have flown back to oppose the trade in charcoal, to plant, and to water young trees. Then they have returned and settled into Minnesota.

*   *   *

With aid from wise teachers, from the people indigenous to our current locations, we can move forward. We can make slow steps toward actions that sustain life.

Any seed may sprout. Someone's grandchild may end up in this yard in Minnesota, eat a cherry from this tree, and be nourished.

* * *

Two things to remember:

When you are in trouble, stop to drink water.

We are owned by our surrounding land and water. Our health depends on theirs.

* * *

Climate change stresses most of us, but working with the soil can give us relief.

During the overwarm Minnesota winter of 2017—which was then followed by an overcold spring of 2018—I asked my friend Bonnie what practices helped her cope with the inconsistencies of our new winters. "Working in my yard," she said. "The daily intimacy of being close to it for so long. I've planted these things and I notice how they are doing. I notice that they are changing depending on the way the seasons behave. Things I planted are acting differently now than they did ten years ago."

* * *

In 2014, on the bus from Minnesota to the People's Climate March in New York City, I met Najwa Bukhari. She, with her husband and young son, could easily have flown; instead they rode that bumpy, crowded bus, as the others did, by choice.

After the march, she agreed to speak with my students. She had been a physician in Saudi Arabia, her home country, where she had led an effort to save the mangrove forests there. At a time when it was not legal in Saudi for more than three people to gather in public, she managed to get permission for women (most of them of a more leisured class) and men (mostly fishermen) to come together for public mangrove-cleaning events.

Roberto, a student in the first class Najwa visited, spoke up right away. "My family in Mexico fishes among the mangroves," he said.

"Without the mangroves we would not have fish. But our groves are in danger like yours. People want to cut them down so they can build houses right by the shore."

Najwa told the class that Saudi Arabia once had stretches of forest, that it once had been green. But now rains no longer come. "Once the trees are cut," she said, "the clouds do not return."

"So it has been in Somalia," several in the class agreed. "With no trees to exhale moisture into the air, few clouds develop above them."

"You have trees and rain yet in Minnesota," Najwa told us. "Protect them. They are your life."

"You are Saudi?" an Oromo student asked. "Do you know that your people are buying our land? My people are not wishing to sell, but the land is being taken from us, then sold to the Saudis. Once your people buy it, they grow crops and take them all back to Saudi Arabia. We have no land left to farm. What can you do about that?"

"Is this true?" said Najwa. "I am sorry if that is so. I will look into this. Please, what is your name?"

She did the research and wrote back to that student. "Yes," she wrote, "what you said is quite true, and I am sorry. I apologize for my country." Then she told him what she was doing to advocate back home against this practice of land theft.

The next semester when Najwa visited my class, she said she was learning permaculture design because she wanted to nourish the land for generations to come.

A couple of months later, my friend Julie mentioned that her restorative agriculture initiative in southern Minnesota would be able to expand into a farm-scale model because a major investor had come forward. A determined couple, she said, was offering to buy sixty acres to add to the forty the project already had.

As she described the passion of her investors for testing out large soil-restoring fields, I thought of Najwa and her husband, Tom. Could they be the investors? "Yes!" she said. "You know Najwa? She has incredible power!"

Over the months, Julie reported back how Najwa inspired and pushed and accompanied her, walking the fields, cajoling the South American and Mexican American immigrant farmers, appeasing people of the nearby college town, listening respectfully to affronted neighboring farmers, meeting with lawyers and bankers. She persistently explained to the bankers that, no, she was not interested in protecting the interest on the money for her children—what she was interested in was protecting the land forever for all children on earth. The bankers had never drawn up such a contract before, but Najwa and Julie persisted. What they arrived at was a covenant for the land. In April the purchase agreement was signed. In May Najwa led a ceremony of blessing for the land and saw the first seeds planted. Then she and her family flew back to Saudi Arabia.

* * *

My son's girlfriend's mother gave him a cookbook by Sean Sherman called *The Sioux Chef's Indigenous Kitchen.* I picked it up when I visited them in Seattle. "He's from Minnesota, you know," I said. "His mission is that we all return to indigenous food."

"Pick recipes, Ma," my son said. "We're having a big group for dinner on Saturday. Pick something Minnesotan, something you diabetics can eat, something that will seem like a feast."

I picked out six recipes. They called for things that I knew from home—sumac, bergamot, juniper, duck egg, squash, pumpkin seeds, spruce boughs, blueberry, wild rice, sage, bison.

I walked and bused and ferried through the Seattle area looking for the ingredients we needed. Most of the items were native to the Northwest, too, so I was able to find them, but bergamot—no. And bison we'd have had to preorder. Therefore, as Sherman suggests, we adapted. We substituted beef for the bison and Green Earl Grey Tea for bergamot. *Next time I visit,* I decided, *I'll bring bergamot from my yard.*

As we were preparing that feast, Julie called.

"What are you doing?" she asked.

"Cooking great stuff from the Sioux Chef," I replied.

"Sean Sherman?" she asked. "I'm seeing him for a meeting next week. Send a picture of your meal—he'll be pleased to see it."

*　*　*

In caring for the future, you may have to give up air travel, sweat through hot summer days with minimal AC, and turn down your heat in winter, but you don't have to give up good food.

Not if you forage and plant.

Digging saved my sanity when I was first in climate-induced shock. Planting saved it again as I was gaining back strength after my diabetes diagnosis.

*　*　*

When he was in high school, my son spread a profusion of natives and exotics in our backyard, a wild mess of this here and that there. Then he left for college.

I looked out in confusion.

As I began to dig, I learned to know plants by their roots. The foot-long white rhizomes of the quack grass became my companions, even as I cast them on the stone walk. "You have all the ditches," I'd tell them, "all the edges of rail lines. Here in the garden we make way for prairie dropseed." My fingers followed the white strands of root to the ends. The topsoil clustered and slipped away, moist against my hands.

Contact with dirt healed my spirit. Contact with the ground soothes our bodies and ministers to the land.

Up north, I spent hours following the rhizomes of hawkweed, bagging it in black plastic until it was rotted enough to become compost. My efforts brought me peace. The cleared spaces also allowed some wild strawberry, some violets, and even a moccasin flower to return.

I planted strawberry, plum, and serviceberry bushes for birds.

I dried mint and rose hips, made high-bush cranberry sauce.

And hung out my wash to dry.

I carried water from the lake to young trees.

Contact with soil microbes can relieve depression. I know that it settled my distress and that, when I feel distress again, I can return to the soil to find calm.

More and more of us are learning to create soil. We are walking with greater care over the land, listening to each living neighbor. We are turning our hearts and our ways toward harmony with the fragile fabric of humus and water and life that encircles this globe.

We are giving survival a chance.

And, even if these efforts fail, we will have moved toward light, toward the mystery of life.

*   *   *

Julie called me on a bright day in June to say that Najwa had died at her mother's home in Saudi Arabia.

Before she left Minnesota, Najwa had watched the planting of the first hazelnut bushes. She had helped spread the first wildflower seeds across that land.

Remember Najwa's words about clouds. If the trees are gone, the clouds won't come. With Najwa, protect and plant bushes and trees.

When next I saw Tom, Najwa's husband, he showed me an email from Saudi Arabia. People there had just given a memorial for his wife. For Najwa they had planted fifty trees.

Coming Home

Offer a handful of water to the soil outside
your dwelling. Learn where that water flows.

Remember and honor your natal watershed.

Speak the name of the watershed
that now sustains your life.

Trace its extent on a map.

Connect with people and other animals
and plants who have lived, and who now live,
in this watershed's embrace.

Take action to care for your watershed's flow.
Perhaps you will clean trash from its margins.
Maybe you will plant native grasses and trees
with deep roots. With others, you may remove
a dam and allow a marsh to reappear.
You may walk the length of a river.

Take action to care for those who share this
water with you. Plant berry bushes for its birds.
Pass laws to protect its foxes. Practice
composting with its human children.

14

FOG

Diabetes has made me more comfortable with solitude. It grounds me. I glance at my BG monitor maybe twenty times a day. Each time, I am looking into myself. I contemplate my hands when I prick for a drop of blood.

*   *   *

In 2018, I attended a talk by Kenny Blumenfeld, senior climatologist at the Minnesota State Climate Office. He'd promised to discuss the ways our changing climate is affecting Minnesota.

Blumenfeld began by saying that people make mistakes by conflating local weather with global climate patterns. They also confuse observation with prediction.

New information about climate change, Blumenfeld said, arrives every week. He said we need to stay up to date. What we knew in 2006 is not what climate scientists know now. And, also, he cautioned, we do not know all that we wish to know. No human does. The funding and political will are often not available to support those of us who are trying to learn. Even when they are, human abilities have limits.

* * *

What I know about my diabetic body, three years in, is vastly more than I knew at the start. And what people who have lived with type 1 for decades know makes my store of knowledge a mere spoonful.

Researchers report new conclusions and observations week by week. And even those who read every report, who are on the front lines, do not know everything.

My blood has taught me this—do not panic when high blood sugar numbers report that the liquid flowing through me is harming my organs. Instead, accept the information and adjust: hold back on carbs, drink water, walk, make a correction, change my future behavior.

* * *

So, too, as the temperatures rise, we must accept these realities and adjust: cut back on carbon, care for water, take correction, change the course of the future.

Blumenfeld laid out what we do know. Basically, northern Minnesota is losing the cold of winter. Secondarily, so far, Minnesota is gaining in water—and that water is coming, more and more often, in deluges. Yet drought could come later.

Here is what else he told us:

- The earth's surface temperature increased gradually until 1970, and then rapidly after that.

- The water temperature in the ocean has increased as much as the temperature of the land has.

- Since 1895, Minnesota has seen increasing temperature and precipitation, and those increases have been more pronounced since 1987.

- Northern Minnesota has become warmer by 2.3 degrees Celsius (that's 4.14 degrees Fahrenheit) since 1985, southern

Minnesota has become warmer by 1.1 degrees Celsius
(1.98 degrees Fahrenheit) in that same time.

- Low temperatures are rising faster than high temperatures.

- Since 1970, winter has been warming thirteen times faster
  than summer, and that number keeps getting bigger.

- Northern Minnesota has had some summer warming,
  but not much.

- The southern part of Minnesota has had an actual cooling
  of summertime highs.

- The number of days during which temperatures never drop
  below freezing is rapidly increasing throughout the state.

- The growing season has not gotten longer, but we have
  lost about thirty days of freezing temperatures.

- The decade of the 1960s saw the most reliable turning
  of the seasons in modern recorded time, with the freeze
  days all outside the growing season.

I came of age in that most stable period of seasons—after the
Dust Bowl but before the significant loss of cold. What formed the
foundation of my expectation was the most stable climate in Minnesota's scientifically recorded history.

I grew up in the north, and I came back intermittently enough
to be startled by the changes. People who live in the southern part
of the state have not seen as much change. People who have lived
continuously in the north may have acclimated more gently. For me
to come back in January and find no forty below was a shock; for
them the adjustment may have been gradual.

"What," Blumenfeld asked, "is making winter warmer?" He told
us that we have some warmer days, but not many. What we do not
have are the very cold days. Each decade, the coldest day of winter
has warmed by 1 degree Celsius. That means that the coldest day

has become 1.8 of my dad's kind of degrees warmer each decade. If we had 50 below in 1960, all we'll get, as the very lowest, he said, is 39.2 below by 2020.

I remember 55 below. It wasn't bad for humans—wrapped warmly with a scarf over your face, walking briskly, you'd be as fine as you were at 20 below. And, I want to add, you'd feel a lot warmer than I feel now in places where 40 degrees above comes with drizzle, where cold is accompanied by fog. Our 55 below was dry; you could shake the snow out of your boot, stick your foot back in, and keep it warm.

More important, 55 below was good for red pines, for moose, for people who don't want to be bitten by ticks.

Blumenfeld continued: "The character of winter is changing dramatically on the interior of every continent. In Grand Rapids, Minnesota, we hit 35 below only twice recently."

He showed no emotion when he said that trees are showing stress from too much heat, especially in northern Minnesota—and that some tree species are being pushed out of their usual ranges. The birches, it seems to me, are dying. People say that new trees will take their places, but most trees take a long time to grow, longer than a human takes to live an entire life. How do we expect them to fill a forest if the conditions in that forest continually change?

"Precipitation," Blumenfeld said, "has increased statewide." More snow falls, and spring rains are heavier, but not so much in the far north. He said that water is falling in greater amounts mostly in the southeast and center of the state.

I had worried about the threat of more and stronger tornadoes because of the warmed-up air—but, according to Blumenfeld, those have not happened here.

Good, I think. *Sometimes it's really nice to be wrong.*

I also worried about coming drought. But we haven't had an increase in dry years since 1895. And the droughts we have had—even the one that shook loose my confidence in 1989—have not been worse than they were in the decades before.

Minnesota is getting wetter, not drier. According to Blumenfeld, "It used to be that the heaviest rainfall in Minnesota was six inches, but now it's eleven inches. We've had a stair-step increase in the number of one-inch rainfalls, a 15 or 25 percent increase."

Blumenfeld predicts that two hazards will increase in frequency and intensity in Minnesota by midcentury: flash floods and heat. "We will begin to see extreme heat. A big increase in the number of days above 95," he said, "doubling or tripling the number of such days by midcentury. The best science says we will get hotter, but we don't know when."

I thought of the brush and dry leaves in the valley by the house up north, of the balsam growing on the slope. If it gets to be 95 and if there has been no rain for some weeks . . .

Blumenfeld added, "Additional consecutive dry days are being projected by midcentury, but the research indications for that are weak."

Winter is failing. Because we have failed winter. Because too few people know why they ought to have loved it.

*   *   *

Ogmani came into my office, bowing slightly to me. "Hello, Teacher," he said. I could hear the capital *T*.

The essay he had written had become a love song to Kabul, his home. "A beautiful city," he said, "no matter what you hear in the news."

"Were you born there, Ogmani?" I asked.

"Oh, no," he said. "In a village, even more beautiful. Here, I will show you." He pulled out his phone to show me a picture of a family—grandparents, younger adults, a couple of children—standing smiling in snow.

"They sent this yesterday because they were happy that snow had come. We don't get snow anymore, hardly ever," he said. "That is the problem. Not enough snow for the crops, so most of us have gone to Kabul. That one, the small girl, she is my niece."

I have heard this too often—no longer enough snow. No runoff in the spring. Where there used to be drifts of white now are deep drifts of longing.

I tapped my phone and showed him a video of two of my grand-nieces being pulled on a sled behind a car. "This came to me yesterday, too," I said. "We still get deep snow often in northern Minnesota," I said, "though it doesn't stay as long as it did when I was a child. See how happy my grandnieces are!"

Ogmani laughed as he watched the girls.

"Will you go back?" I asked him.

"I must," he said. "I can't leave my niece there alone. I am afraid for her. She is a girl . . . and the Taliban will come. I will go back and become a politician. I will make things better for her." He looked up with pride. "She reads already. I want her to go to school."

"But you could stay here," I said.

"I could, but I will not," he said. "I expect to die. One day there will be a suicide bomb attack and I will die. Just last week a man blew himself up outside the office where my brother works. Each day when my brothers leave the house, my mother blesses them because that may be the last."

"Could you stay and bring your niece here instead?" I asked.

"I will go back," he said. "Afghanistan is my homeland."

*   *   *

In March 2018, I learned of a conference at the Science Museum of Minnesota called Code Blue for Patient Earth, which was to focus on the effects of climate change on human health as well as on the health of other animals, plants, and the entire globe. I knew I had to go.

"The earth is in multisystem failure," the convener announced. "What," she asked, "are we going to do about it?" I looked around. A couple hundred people. Yes, my lake was in trouble, but here, in this room, I did not have to face that alone.

Michael Mahero, a physician originally from Kenya, spoke of

his experience talking with African mothers and hearing how the changing climate has affected their families. These mothers live where many of my African climate-refugee students come from.

He told us, "Being a recipient of that knowledge from the custodians of the knowledge is one of the most exciting and one of the most heart-wrenching roles a researcher can fill. When people see the animals and the forests disappearing, they know that their ways of life are going to be over."

I came to this conference because it linked personal diagnoses with the diagnosis affecting the earth. Rachel Kerr, a nursing instructor, spoke of her home on the Texas Gulf Coast. At the time of Hurricane Katrina, she was newly licensed as a nurse. Suddenly, she said, she was surrounded by a flood of refugees. Fires broke out in New Orleans. People touched metal objects and got electrical shocks. Hospital staff didn't have food for their patients. Thousands arrived in Houston as refugees from those hospitals. And not only patients; medical staff came as refugees, too.

Kerr and others tried to care for all of them; they could not. When Rachel went home after work, she saw refugees across the street from her apartment overflowing from the Astrodome. The people lived there on the streets for weeks, with no bathrooms and little food.

Three years later, when Hurricane Ike struck, Rachel Kerr was six months pregnant with her first baby and had a heart condition that was made worse by heat. The temperature in her apartment rose to 95, and then to 100; she had no air-conditioning. Sick as she was, she had to go to work because at the hospital she would be fed and kept cool. Water was scarce, and what was available had to be boiled before it could be used.

Kerr left Houston and came to Minnesota.

But not everyone could flee. Rachel's parents had to stay. When Hurricane Harvey struck in 2017, her father was unable to travel for six weeks, so he missed his biweekly IV infusions. His health drastically worsened.

When she arrived in Minnesota, Rachel Kerr and other students conducted a survey to see how much information about climate change the students in health professions were getting. Of the students surveyed, 53 percent said their patients were strongly impacted by climate change, but only 1 percent said there was material on climate change in what they studied.

That has begun to change. In 2019, all students in health profession programs at the University of Minnesota began receiving content about the health effects of climate change.

*   *   *

In the material handed out at the conference, I read this: "People with preexisting medical conditions, such as asthma, are particularly sensitive to climate change impacts on air quality. People who have diabetes or who take medications that make it difficult to regulate body temperature are sensitive to extreme heat." That is certainly true in my case; the heat-regulating functions of my body are less adept than they were before.

I also read this: "The effects of climate change also affect people's mental health. In particular, climate- or weather-related disasters can increase the risk of adverse mental health consequences, especially if they result in damage to homes and livelihoods or loss of loved ones. The mental health impacts of these events can range from minimal stress and distress symptoms to clinical disorders, such as anxiety, depression, and post-traumatic stress."

When I read "loss of loved ones," I paused. Were the writers thinking only of people? Winter is a loved one. Moose are loved ones. Birch trees and red pines, too. My lake and all that lives within are loved ones.

*   *   *

When my father fed the birds, he spread black oil sunflower seeds into a feeder by his dining room deck window. At night, flying squirrels would sometimes come. They liked his seed, but he did not like them. He could not see their beauty the way he could the birds'. Worse, they peed on the seed.

He shot them. My dad, who couldn't kill a deer.

I protested: "They wouldn't come if you didn't lure them with seeds. They were here first. We moved in on top of them."

He acquiesced this far—he did not shoot them if I was at the house. When I visited, he would hide his gun.

I wondered whether, perhaps, I might be wrong, so I opened my laptop and searched for "flying squirrel."

"What's this newfangled stuff?" Dad protested when I showed him the page. "You trust these words when they aren't even connected by a cord to anything?"

But he read what I had found. The trees in Dad's beloved boreal forest depend on the mushrooms and other fungi under the top layer of soil. Without a healthy spread of communities beneath the surface, the trees would not be able to take in nutrients. In short, they would die.

Since those essential fungi stay in one place and need help to reproduce, they send out truffle-like bodies (eggs and sperm, more or less) that smell very good to fast-footed creatures like flying squirrels.

Those squirrels dig into the topsoil, eat the tasty fungi bits, run to other parts of the forest, and defecate. Their poop pollinates the mushrooms in that part of the woods and—hurrah!—the trees are saved.

Dad pushed the computer back at me and scratched his head. "Humph!" he said.

He got my brother Greg to make a lid for the bird feeder, so he could close it down at night.

*　　*　　*

The next semester Ogmani, no longer my student, stopped by my office. "Hello, Teacher," he said.

"Ogmani! So glad to see you! But . . . you've shaved your head."

He looked away. "For my brother," he said. "Last month there was a bomber. My brother survived the attack . . . for a day."

"May you be well, Ogmani," I said as he turned to go, "and your niece and your brothers. I will think of you."

"*Insha'Allah.*" A bow.

Then he was gone.

*　　*　　*

Talk of sulfide mining in the north woods has returned. Most environmentalists say it should not be permitted. The Boundary Waters, they say, must be preserved for our grandchildren.

I do not wish for the mines in these forests either, but I am no longer only on the side of the environmentalists. The minerals that the mines would provide are needed for solar panels, catalytic converters, cancer treatment, and my diabetes treatment devices. Shall we give these up? I look at the copper wire every six days when I pull my continuous glucose monitor from my thigh. Could it perhaps be recycled? So far, there is no way. I throw it in the trash and snap a new copper filament into my leg.

We in the United States have no other nearby source for these minerals. After environmental impact statements, public testimony, votes, and agency review, the first mine that would sit just over the hill, in the Lake Superior watershed, is poised to open. Mining under our lake could be next.

Research says that the mining will destroy the waters. But climate change is already doing that job.

When I mention the threat of climate change in the Boundary Waters to antimining activists, they shake their heads. "I know," they say. "The forests will become grassland."

True—for a while. The climate will change and then keep on changing. That grassland will dry out and burn. If the winds alter their course and the rains do not come, there will be little fresh water in the north. Water does not flow into our state, only out of it.

Maybe, if enough of us get to work, we can stop the heating at the grassland phase.

As for sulfide, it's already here. The abandoned taconite mine pits did not miraculously sprout topsoil once the mining stopped. They filled with water and that water leached through the crushed rocks that already contained sulfide ores. So, the waters in those lakes are sulfur filled. Half of the lakes in our woods are mine pit lakes; most of those are sulfured. Sulfide waters aren't coming. They are here.

*　　*　　*

Perhaps the miners and the environmentalists will never like each other.

Those who discovered how to make and dose insulin did not like each other either.

Frederick Banting and John Macleod, the benefactor who offered Banting a working space, aired their hatred for one another publicly, even refusing to accept the 1923 Nobel Prize in Medicine together.

Just the same, their partnership extended millions of lives.

Even if we dislike each other and disagree, we in Minnesota must work together for the water. We are the upstream caretakers. Waters arrive here, mostly pure, from the sky. Four continental river systems receive that water from us. Whether the water we send on is healthy depends on us.

*　　*　　*

Friends and family from my hometown need work. Some hope the mines will give them that work. The company that would mine the sulfide ores nearest our town reports that, if it is allowed to open this mine in our watershed, the extraction will create 650 permanent jobs. Many people in town believe they will get those jobs.

But when I spoke with representatives of the mining industry, I learned that their future employees will need an AA degree at minimum. "No longer," the official said, "can you get a job in a mine with a high school degree. We don't dig out ore by hand or with driver-operated trucks. Computers dig the ore; miners program the computers."

Folks I know in my hometown are not rushing to get degrees; they are waiting for jobs to come and expecting that their (or their parents') mining pasts will qualify them for those jobs.

My climate-refugee students are earning degrees. Would they be welcome as miners in my hometown?

My siblings are trying other tactics to support both the earth and humans. One brother builds houses and tests for household mold. Safe homes will be needed. My sister supports her husband as he oversees the building of a light-rail line in Seattle.

My other brother is an environmental engineer working on nature-based, economical ways to take sulfate out of already impaired waters. He has set up an experimental system on the edge of a mine pit lake, eight miles away from our childhood home as the crows fly, but nearly forty as the pickup drives. He is using swamp bacteria to eat the sulfate and turn it into fertilizer and bits of stone. He plans to restore water in which wild rice can grow.

15

MIRACLES, MYSTERY, AND DREAMS

Diabetes interrupts sleep.

You can't go to sleep until your blood sugar is okay. If it's too low, you have to eat. If it's too high, you have to bolus or walk or drink water (or all three), and then you can't go to sleep until you're sure you haven't done too much of any of those things. If your body and your diabetes are like mine, you can't go to sleep anyway if your numbers are high—your body just won't relax.

Then, once you're asleep, the drama continues. If you're on a pump, and new to it, it wakes you. *Battery low*, it bleeps. *BG meter now*, it reads. *Low predicted*, it warns you. And then, when you take care of that impending low by popping a few glucose tabs (and wondering if you need to get up to brush your teeth again), *High predicted*, it soon reports.

At the start there were other challenges. My infusion site hurt if I lay on it. The sensor (which looks like an inch-and-a-half-long, white, firmly attached wood tick) pulled and burned. Each time I rolled over onto the pump itself, I'd wake up: *What's this hard thing in my bed?* And when I'd get up to pee, it would dislodge from whatever piece of clothing I had attached it to and drop suddenly to hang from its tubing, banging against my leg and pulling on the cannula inserted into my belly.

If my sudden movement pulled the cannula entirely out, I'd have to turn on the light, open my insertion kit, get a new set, jab it in, and remember how to fill the cannula when the canister wasn't being replaced. And then I had to test again, because who knows what that exertion might have done to my sugar? Only then could I return to bed and turn out the light.

And go back to sleep.

The first year or so, I couldn't. But now I can.

*   *   *

One night I dreamed that the system-down moment had come.

Leaving my cat, Earl Grey, in the car, the windows partly down, I parked on an overlook by the Pacific and walked toward a retreat center that I knew had a gathering of planners. As I approached the steps leading to the center, I felt the ground tremble.

I turned back to my car to rescue my cat, but already the guardrail between the parking lot and the ocean cliff had slipped down the incline. The car next to mine began to slide. I watched a woman run toward it, grab hold, and skid with it over the edge. My own car jolted and tilted seaward. My cat jumped to the window, calling for me.

I paused. If I ran to rescue him, I also would go into the gap. My duty was to warn the organizers that the collapse had begun. They should, I thought, tell people to settle into meditation because it would be futile to flee.

I looked at Earl, trusted that he would remember that I loved him, and turned away. I hurried down the steps and over the walkways, even as they crumbled behind me, toward the center where the leaders, sitting in a plenary, did not wish to be disturbed. I pounded on the door anyway and told them how the ground was slipping. Then I settled into my breath.

I woke up.

Earl purred near me. I made my morning tea.

* * *

It was the middle of the night when Frederick Banting discovered a path toward isolating the substance that would extend the lives of people with diabetes. He had spent a long day preparing for a lecture and poring over a medical article about the pancreas. When he went to bed, he couldn't sleep. "I thought about the lecture and about the article and I thought about my miseries and how I would like to get out of debt and away from worry," he wrote later. "Finally, about two in the morning after the lecture and the article had been chasing each other through my mind for some time, the idea occurred to me." That idea led to the identification of insulin.

For the miraculous fortune of type 1 folks, Banting could not sleep that night.

* * *

At a writer's residency at the Mesa Refuge in Point Reyes Station, California, I looked through my writing shed window toward the San Andreas Fault. Quail skittered on the ground. The boughs of a cypress flowed with the wind. Red-tailed hawks floated by. Owls hooted. The day before, I had walked beneath bluebirds.

The land under me was the North American shelf. Across, a mile away, lay the Pacific shelf. One day, predictions holding, these two will gyrate.

An earthquake is not climate change, though some months before a neighbor had told me that ocean scientists are finding that the increased weight of water in the ocean is not raising the shoreline as quickly as they had expected. Instead, the newly thawed water is pushing down the floor of the ocean. "Imagine," my neighbor said, "what that's doing to the tectonic plates."

I looked out on those tectonic plates. We will die, one way or another. Until that day comes, let us protect any bluebirds we can.

*　*　*

In the week after Typhoon Haiyan hit the Philippines in 2013, killing at least 6,300 humans (I don't know how many butterflies and goats), Anna Mary visited my global studies class. Anna Mary had left her home near Tacloban, Philippines, when she was fifteen; now she worked at our college. She helped people find housing when they were homeless, food when they were hungry, suits when they were interviewing for jobs.

She told our class that, the night before, she had made phone contact with her father and that, God be praised!, he was safe. The cousins she had heard from so far were alive, though their houses were gone.

She asked the class to remember children who were suddenly without parents and parents who were now without their children. She said she would be sending a box on a boat—"There is no rush," she assured us. "The contents will be needed in six months as much as they are needed today"—and suggested we donate coloring books and other things to keep the children busy while they waited for their upended lives to mend.

My student Elijah stood up. We knew him for his fierce independence and his outrage at oil spills ruining farmlands in his homeland of Nigeria. He offered twenty dollars. "Please, buy for the children," he said to Anna Mary.

Delora was next with her twenty. Anna Mary's eyes brimmed over. Delora hugged her.

Delora was a retired army captain in her forties. In her youth, she had joined the service as a path out of the violence of a Chicago neighborhood. A year before the typhoon, she had written about her boot camp experience in the "gas chamber"—the hut she and other recruits were required to enter so they could learn how to move through a fog of poisonous air. Delora had gasped her way out of that hut. She was proud that she survived, proud that she was tougher than her family thought she could be.

But then, Delora developed asthma.

When she began reading the global studies class material, she clicked on every link offered by the online text and filled my in-box with her insights. Sitting front center in the classroom, she alternately coughed and asked questions.

I wished, sometimes, that she would let up. Once when she stopped by my office, I suggested that she needed more rest. I noticed that her cough did not go away.

The Sunday after Anna Mary visited our class, I spoke at my Quaker meeting of the good we can find even when dire challenges confront our earthly home. I told the group gathered about Delora and her twenty-dollar gift.

The next day she wasn't in class.

*   *   *

Back in my office, I opened my in-box. Two messages leapt out, one labeled "RE: Delora Gray" and one from Delora herself.

The counseling office message told me that Delora was dead. She had been found by police that morning after her family reported that she was not answering their calls. She had died reaching for her inhaler. Her hand had fallen short.

The message from Delora said, *"Hello, teacher! This class is changing my life. I saw the world in the army but I didn't know anything about it. Now I have a purpose. I will be an ambassador for global studies. Nothing will stop me. See you soon. Delora."*

*   *   *

One day I asked a new group of students to write what they hoped to be doing in twenty years. Most of them didn't even pick up their pens.

I said, "Didn't you hear what I asked?"

"Ranae," said a young man in the back, "we won't be alive in twenty years."

"Twenty years isn't many," I said.

"We've heard what's happening to the earth," another one said. "We aren't going to last."

"Okay," I said, "but what if you do? Shouldn't you be prepared just in case?"

Twenty years may have been too many to ask young people to plan for. Despair is not a country where they should live.

Next time, I'll ask them to imagine five.

*　*　*

Early in my climate distress, I walked out onto the frozen lake on a January afternoon. I held out my hands to the lake, full of agony because of the crumbling life support systems, because of the thawing of the poles.

Suddenly I heard words. Those words said, "Quiet yourself. You will live to see the return of the cold."

I was comforted, my agony silenced.

Miracles are possible. Not going-against-nature miracles, but we-don't-understand-this-yet miracles.

In the meantime, our visions, our dreams, our efforts, and our restful breathing offer relief.

16

WHEN THE TIME COMES

I asked a diabetes nurse educator, "If the system were to collapse, what am I to do?" She looked at me blankly.

"For example," I said, "if I were living in Syria right now."

Her look grew puzzled. "You'd go to the nearest emergency room."

"In Syria?" I said.

Later I asked a different nurse educator the same question.

She nodded. "Before insulin, people stayed alive for some time on diets of protein and vegetables with very little carbohydrate," she told me. "You wouldn't live long, but you could live awhile."

Soon after, I asked my endocrinologist. She looked at me flatly and replied, "Remember how you felt before you came to the ICU?"

"Yes, I do," I said.

"You would feel like that," she told me. "You would live for maybe four hours, maybe two days. It isn't a painful death. You'd go to sleep. Your heart would stop."

Two days. Not many.

"But the system isn't likely to go down," she said.

* * *

Marie, an African American grandmother who lives on the Northside of Minneapolis, had taken my global studies class and my research writing class. She was one of nine students— Somali, Oromo, Native American, Euro-American, and African American—who volunteered to speak of their firsthand experiences with climate disruption at a national gathering of people who were working toward sustainable lifestyles.

"In the past four months," Marie told those who came to listen, "I've experienced twenty deaths. It's been hard to get my classwork done because I've been so sad. Almost everyone died of cancer or asthma. I think these diseases are all caused by climate change, or at least by the environment."

Asthma, I had told her, has direct links to climate change. Many cancers may be environmentally caused as well. "You could research that," I had said.

She didn't have time, she told me. "Anyway, isn't the garbage burner just down the street from my apartment?"

Other students described climate devastation in their homelands. Those listening were activists working to limit ecological harm, but they had not, before this, interacted directly with people who had watched their watersheds fail, their soil crack open. One woman almost left the room because what she heard was too painful for her. "Just in time," she told me, "you let us each go talk with one of the presenters."

* * *

We have been trying so hard to extend individual lives that we have damaged our home.

Many of the people I grew up with shake their heads sadly and say, "We must leave this in the hands of God. God is powerful. God's will shall prevail."

I wish to say, "*We* are the hands of God. You and I. What will we do for Marie's neighbors?"

* * *

In Puerto Rico during the weeks following Hurricane Maria, few people had electric power. Many had no running water. In their thirst, some drank from sewers. The people with type 1 there struggled to keep their insulin cool.

Even we folks here on the U.S. mainland were affected by the storm. My pump supplies were backordered; I read in the news that the Medtronic factories on the island could not function without power.

* * *

We type 1 people cannot live without insulin. Ecological and social and infrastructure stability are required to support the flow of insulin to us. Without insulin, our blood sugar will soar; our hearts will be damaged; we will enter diabetic ketoacidosis; and we will likely have strokes. In an ecological disaster, emergency rooms will be overwhelmed.

I began to keep a two-month supply of insulin in the fridge. I ordered an insulated carrier to pack my supply with me. I froze enough ice to last two weeks. I considered that the small pond in my backyard might stay cool at the bottom. That deep, cool lake might be needed, even in the city.

I researched other ways for diabetics like me to survive. People did survive for a time with type 1 diabetes in the decades before the role of insulin was discovered. A man named Dr. Frederick Allen found dietary ways to let people with diabetes—Elizabeth Hughes, for example—live for up to three years.

* * *

If a system breakdown occurs, I will first gather up the supplies I have. I'll stretch them out, staying on my pump as long as I can because it helps me use less insulin.

I'll keep what insulin is unopened in a cool, deep hole, or at the bottom of some lake, or in my evaporative bag, or inside a thick gourd.

I will eat sparingly of protein—an egg, if possible—and noncarb vegetables, and I'll walk after eating. I'll rest, if I can, between meals. If I must be physically active, I'll eat any seeds or nuts I can find.

To conserve test strips and battery power, I'll test only once a day; to conserve insulin, I'll correct only if my blood glucose numbers are above 200.

When my insulin runs out, I'll try to bring my numbers down by drinking water and walking.

Then, when the time comes, I'll go to sleep.

*   *   *

Each bite we take, some lettuce or chicken or bean sprout has died and is reborn into us.

Let us allow death. Let us prepare for life to go on.

People are dying of climate-related stress in Syria, in Mongolia, in Puerto Rico, on the Northside of Minneapolis. Wolves and moose and warblers and bears and butterflies and sea lions and coral and sphagnum mosses are passing away.

Yet, many are searching for a way. A man in Siberia is trying to re-create the great northern grass fields, complete with woolly mammoth, to keep the permafrost from melting. Farmers in the United States are developing restorative agriculture to create carbon-catching soil banks. Ocean habitat creators are making vertical structures to support dozens of interdependent ecosystems. The best and wisest among us are working toward solutions.

We may be despairing about the climate cascade. Yet desperation has been known to lead to relief.

*   *   *

Hold to rocks, to stars, to wind. These things will remain.

At this moment, the precious body breathes; the scarred Earth pulses with life. At this moment, legs move, and, somewhere, birds call through leafy trees.

In this moment, before the next wave of collapse, we are alive.

This is the moment we have. Now. This is the only moment we have.

What is the opening, here, at this time?

Listen and Prepare

When messages from your own body echo those coming from the larger web of life, take note.

Is your breathing troubled? What, then, is happening to the air surrounding the nearby trees?

Is your digestion unsettled? What is happening this day to the life-forms in the food you eat and in the water you drink?

Are you thirsty? What living beings around you are longing for water too?

Consider that smog is fog laced with smoke and that it chokes birds along with humans. When a virus attacks our lungs, those whose lungs have been damaged by smog often give way first.

Attempt to relieve strains on the life systems around you as you strive for your own health.

In quiet wisdom, make your system-down plan. Then, set it aside until the day of need.

Practice giving over to sleep and to dreams.

For now, live. Breathe. Be. Be with.

17

RETURN

Spring

On my birthday, Dad fell.

He was ninety years old. He had been overseeing the tilling of his garden. When he reached the house again and bent to turn off the hose, he fell. "Oi!" he called to Mom. "Sweetheart, come help me up."

Mom saw his shoulder blade sticking out sideways and told him to lie still.

In the hospital, Dad asked me to look at his back. He had to be helped to lift his right side. The blood had pooled and turned black across the entire expanse; the green bruise was spreading. I could see that he would soon die.

He did not expect to go to heaven. He would await resurrection.

The October before, we had sat at the kitchen table and watched leaves fluttering down. He had said, "The leaves fall. They decompose. Something new grows out of them. I think it might be like that. Something else grows out of our lives."

We promised Dad that he could die at home, so we brought him to the lake in an ambulance. He moaned as the paramedics jostled the stretcher down the thirty-four stone steps he had laid to the door.

We set up his bed in front of the window. We showed him the view of the lake. He attempted a smile.

For four more hours he lived. Then, my brother Greg beside him, he let out the last of his breath.

Summer

Dad had signed up to be cremated. He hadn't liked that idea—it would be harder for Jesus to collect all the parts when he returned if they had mostly gone up in smoke. However, Dad's God was a God of miracles, and this would not be His first.

So, once the cremation society had done its work, Dad's urn, made by Greg of cedar wood from our lot at the lake, sat in front of the window facing the water. He was near the lake all summer as the waters changed from quiet to wild, from white to black, from evening pink to morning beige.

We would place him in the ground when the time was right.

* * *

After Dad died, worried for children and alarmed for all life, I took myself to the woods. Winding through the scrub poplar and hazel brush, trekking past drying fern, up and down the slight rises, I followed a path made by deer. I walked near the hollow where I had visited a wolf-killed deer the winter before. Half a mile later, I arrived at the oldest white pine on that tract of land. It rose above the surrounding woods, nodding to the distant pines and the few tall spruce that stood out above the rest.

I sat against it, leaning my back into its broad bark. It surprised me with movement. I looked up through the delicate lace of its needles, far to the blue sky above. There was wind, moving it, coursing all the way down to the base, there where my back settled against it.

Relaxing into its sway, I prayed to the tree: "Please, take care of my daughter." I did not expect a reply, did not think the tree could hear me, assumed I was merely wishing.

But I heard a reply. The tree said, "If you will take care of mine."

Pinecones open only during fire, and I knew that no fires had been allowed in these woods for the past forty-five years. Therefore, this tree could not have a daughter.

I stood up, unnerved. I walked away from the tree, pushing farther into the brush. And then I was pulled up short by a blur of white pine needle.

Just a little taller than I was, a young white pine stood. Forty feet from her mother. The daughter of the pine, struggling to grow amid a tangle of other thin trunks.

I turned back to the old one. "Yes," I said. "I will take care of yours."

*   *   *

Now, when I return to the lake, I consider what Dad would say about the threats—the failing of winter, the possibility of a copper mine under the water. About climate change I think he would be clear: "God is stronger than man," he would say. After a pause, he'd consider and add, "And yet, we can make a mess of things, sure."

"Don't fret, Ranae," he'd go on. "God is still in control. Springtime and harvest, He's promised them to us. Remember? Genesis 8:22: 'While the earth remaineth, seedtime and harvest, and cold and heat, and summer and winter, and day and night shall not cease.' God spoke that to Noah, and God is still in control."

I'm glad Dad won't be here when winter fully abandons his woods.

About the copper mining, I think he'd just shake his head. "Don't know about these big companies," he'd say. "They just better do it right. We sure could use some good solar panels. Remember that first one I bought for the house? I hear they make them better now."

Fall

My brother Jeff opened his computer and searched. The internet said that we could find a place called Birch Lake Cemetery across our bay and to the east of Perch Lake, close to a hillside where we had camped. It was, he read, the resting place of original settlers in the area.

Jeff and my mother drove down an unpaved road off the Blueberry Cutoff, came to a marker with "Hanson's Crossing" carved into it, turned back a bit, and found the lane to the cemetery. Between a small nut-shaped lake called Hanson's and another small double-bay lake called Pearl, on the top of a mounded portion of land, they found a sparsely filled cemetery surrounded by a chain-link fence.

They walked in and up to the tallest white pine. Near it stood a flagpole and also a wooden bench where a person could sit to contemplate the log barn across the bay, the lilies in the lake, the herons overhead.

Jeff met the couple who owned the farm and barn across Pearl Lake. They explained that the cemetery had been deeded to a Lutheran church in Ely so that no one could ever develop it. They said that, sure, we could bury Dad's ashes there. We just needed to pick out a spot.

Mom chose the place at the top, under the boughs of the white pine where a view of water sparkled through the green needles.

The people who first built houses on the north side of Birch Lake had set aside this cemetery. It holds folks not accepted at the graveyards in Ely—some Finnish immigrants who were kicked out of the mines because they tried to start unions, and some Ojibwe Finnish folks who were not traditional enough to be buried on the reservation and not white enough to be buried in town.

Unmarked graves lie there too, indicated only by flat stones sunk sideways into the earth around small rectangular plots—children, I expect, whose names are forgotten.

It was the right place for us. Here, Dad would be in good company, near moose and visited by wolves.

* * *

Fall arrived before we could all gather to say our goodbyes. Almost all of our cousins came. My siblings. Grandchildren. We held the big funeral at a church in the town of Embarrass, but the graveside service was for family alone. Two ministers came. The director of ministry from my Quaker meeting walked quietly among the trees and stood at the back, not speaking at all. The minister from the Assembly of God in town came. We siblings had huddled with him ahead of time and said that, while he was welcome, we would be the only ones to speak.

My brothers and the grandsons had dug a hole the day before. I handed around the shawl that Dad's mother had crocheted, the one that had lain over the back of his chair, so each of the cousins could hold it a moment before we wrapped it round the cedar urn. Dad would be warm.

Almost everyone spoke at the graveside—the farm cousins, the Bemidji cousins, we descendants of Dad, and Mother. We stood in a circle under that pine and did what our ancestors had trained us to do. We each spoke as God gave us words.

I told them what Grandpa had told me to say, why our family is listed as Heathen in Denmark.

And then we passed the shovel and covered Dad up.

* * *

The next day, I returned to my own white pines with a nephew and a handsaw. We cut out most of the saplings that were crowding the young pine. We gave it space, sunlight, and air.

When next I went back to Dad's cemetery, I found wolf hair on the gate where someone had spent time scratching.

Winter

I step into my sheep-wool-lined boots and set out to visit the white pines.

My time is short, my diabetes demanding. I've packed a fifteen-carb sesame snack and a packet of emergency sugar wafers—enough, I think, for a hike of less than a mile.

The snow is crusted below the soft top. Because only a few deer have passed through recently, that crust breaks awkwardly every third step I take. Dropping down into the powder takes more energy than I reckoned. I eat the sesame snack early on.

A woodpecker knocks up ahead. I lurch awkwardly along the path. Once, to rest, I lie on the snow. Blue, blue sky above. Air clean and cold.

Then I go on. I find the young pine has grown taller. A spruce, the only one I spared, is perhaps crowding it, but also, perhaps, a companion during the winds. I touch the young pine and go on to the mother.

"My daughter, like yours, is well," I tell her. "Thank you."

I sit next to her. She is not moving this time.

I check my blood glucose monitor. Quite low. I could get into trouble. I eat my remaining sugar wafers. I suspend my insulin feed.

I have to get back. To fall in the woods would be foolish, even if I want more time with this tree.

Near my hand is a slanted stick. I reach for it. Loose. I take it. With it as a walking pole, my feet will not slide into each crusty hole.

A wren chirps to my left. I set out toward the house. Clouds lower; I nod to a frosty fog that hangs over Minnow Lake.

Just before my sugar bottoms out, I arrive. But barely. I have eaten exactly enough food, taken not too many steps, found a sturdy companion stick.

We are looking out for one another's children, that tall white pine and I.

Spring

I will keep going back. Sulfide mining may harm the waters. Climate change will replace the tamaracks with grass. Our moose will die. Loons may no longer come. Doubtless, new refugees will arrive. Yet, as long as water falls from the sky, that lake will spread from its banks. As long as I am able, I will return to its shores.

Water washes through us. Water gives us life. Water waits.

18

MAY YOUR WATERSHED LIVE— AND YOU WITH IT

None of us has the luxury of resting, complacent, into the benefi-
cent care of our watersheds. Today, every flow is threatened.

Yet, everywhere, green shoots struggle to break through dry soil.
In your life, in your heart, water is flowing. Reach out to it.

1. Stop. Just stop. Look around. What is here? *Where did the
   water wash away the topsoil? Could a rain garden go there?
   Maybe a dishpan to catch some of the torrent?*
2. Then breathe. After some breaths, make a plan for restoring
   your place. Pick up fallen branches; water trees; find a cool
   place; walk to a nearby water source.
3. Listen to other beings and watch the flow of the streams.
   Consult elders who know this land. Perhaps they will say, "Run
   from this place because the rivers are going." Perhaps they will
   say, "Stay put. Mother Earth is rebalancing. Trust her."
4. When grief comes, as it will, and when sorrow flows, allow.

But put limits around your tears. There are people younger and more vulnerable who need companions. Be present to them and show them ways to care for their waters.

5. Build community across barriers. Consider all means, natural and technological, to support the water of life. Choose the ones that might work.

6. Tell others of your efforts, your joys, and your griefs. Listen fully as they tell you theirs. Carry the stories of those who are not present, whose words you remember. Birds also wish their messages to be heard.

7. Walk out into the world. Check on a neighbor tree and on a stream of water. Clean refuse from a storm sewer's grate. Pick up plastic before it reaches the sea.

8. If but a sliver of ground shows, push down a seed, share water with what sprouts. If no space outside seems suitable, grow herbs in your home. Care for soil and plants. Listen for what the near watershed asks of you.

9. Sleep with awareness of soil and sand and stones beneath. Practice letting go. Let dreams open a path into and then through this place and this time. Remember that from the unknown, joyous possibilities may flow.

10. Allow death. Yet, as long as your eyes can open, as long as your breath lasts, live deeply in your own particular place as a part of the watershed upon which your life depends.

Being here, being aware, may allow your waters to flow.

Remember the Branches and Stones

Stop →
Survey the situation →
Breathe →
Practice following cycles of care →
Listen →
Settle to return to your body and your watershed →
Feel →
Grieve; amend; turn around →
Connect →
Value, with humility, both nature and science →
Witness →
Retell what the Earth and the water-deprived say →
Walk →
Nourish those who depend on your watershed →
Water →
Plant; create soil; map your watershed →
Sleep →
Allow miracles and mystery →
Live until death →
Leave gently when the time arrives.

CODA

Life Principles of the Ojibwe People Indigenous to Northern Minnesota Watersheds

Winona LaDuke

The way things are in nature is the way things ought to be.

Life moves in cycles and ought to move in cycles.

Nearly everything is alive.

We are all one family.

All that lives has standing, even to the furthest generations.

We should take what we need and leave the rest.

When we take, we must give.

The Good Life leads to continual rebirth.

ACKNOWLEDGMENT

I give thanks to this earth and its interdependent beings—to all the trees, waters, winds, moving beings, and still beings who have welcomed me to life. This book is yours.

You people who have contributed are beyond number. You are each precious to me. I am grateful that we are together in life, in story, and in renewal.

Special thanks to Scott Edelstein, the editor who told me to braid the strands. Deep thanks to Kristian Tvedten, my editor at the University of Minnesota Press, who believed this book would find willing readers. In gratitude to all at Minneapolis College and at the University of Minnesota Press, I pass on what you have generously given to me.

NOTES

HOW TO LIVE

page xvii: This title will, I hope, raise the question for you. I do not know how you should live; I can only share hints that life and those I have encountered have offered me.

In *Diabetes Rising: How a Rare Disease Became a Modern Pandemic, and What to Do about It* (Kaplan Publishing, 2010), Dan Hurley presents the history of, possible causes of, and attempted responses to (aiming toward cures for) diabetes in both types. He focuses on the U.S. situation but includes the worldwide impact. He calls diabetes a global pandemic, though, technically, it is not a pandemic because it is not contagious.

1. WHERE WATERS DIVIDE

page 1: "Each child's fate": Many humans and other animals move from watershed to watershed over the course of their lives. Often that move is caused by the drying out or destruction of the watershed into which they were born. Most immigrant students whose stories I tell moved because of situations caused by watershed distress.

page 2: "an acre they had purchased for stumpage": Stumpage is the right to

cut and sell the trees on a section of woods purchased by a person
from someone else who legally owns that land.

page 4: "I remember feathers": A family picture has recently emerged that
shows my young brother on this man's knee. Two eagle feathers rise from
the breast pocket of the Red Lake leader's shirt.

page 5: "near a town called Trail": The land my grandfather homesteaded was
Ojibwe land. The people's roads crossed near or through his farm. I do
not know whether Grandpa knew he was participating in the destruction of Ojibwe lives and culture by fencing the land, plowing the forests,
and shooting the animals that had been at home there. His government
praised his industry.

page 26: "The atmospheric CO_2 levels in 1970": A full explanation of atmospheric carbon dioxide levels and methods of measuring them can be
found at the Global Monitoring Laboratory at https://www.esrl.noaa.gov
/gmd/ccgg/trends.

2. DO NOT FALL AWAY

page 31: "But the lakes I had canoed on": The land we built our house on was,
at first, leased from the state of Minnesota. In the 1990s, the state sold
that near-acre of land to our family. Our land, along with our hometown
of Babbitt, is surrounded by the Superior National Forest. In 1978 the
million-acre Boundary Waters Canoe Area Wilderness (BWCAW) was
established in the forest, cutting off the free access people in the area had
enjoyed but also adding further protected status to those acres. A map
of the forest is available at https://www.fs.usda.gov/Internet/FSE_MEDIA
/stelprdb5130373.pdf.

3. PAUSE TO SURVEY

page 37: "A grandfather from North Minneapolis": Unless a person whose
stories I tell has asked me to use her or his actual name, I have changed
those names. The stories remain, essentially, as they were given to me.
As a teacher I focused on supporting my students to tell their own
stories; however, those students often requested that I use my privileges
to tell wider audiences what they shared with me.

CONSIDER THE NEED TO STOP

page 45: As the brick walls of the college would not have protected my students and me if the gun had fired, so the parts of life that usually protect (forests, coastlines, glaciers) have begun to shatter as the climate cracks. Knowing this, we are obligated to respond.

4. THE PATTERN OF BREATH

page 49: "The moose were dying": Brent McDonald, "Minnesota Mystery: What's Killing the Moose?" *New York Times,* March 5, 2014, https://www.nytimes.com/2014/03/06/us/minnesota-mystery-whats-killing-the-moose.html.

page 51: "the cause of the decline in Minnesota moose": Minnesota Department of Natural Resources, 2018 Aerial Moose Survey now included in https://files.dnr.state.mn.us/wildlife/moose/moosesurvey.pdf, a 2020 report.

STOP. BREATHE. SETTLE.

page 55: A great number of students at our college, and of immigrants worldwide, are ecological (often climate) refugees. Recognizing that the troubles that precipitated flight from a homeland arose from drought or tsunami or hurricane or wildfire can unsettle established assumptions.

5. THIRST

page 60: "In 1970, twice as many wild animals": Information about the percentage of land animals that are wild comes from Peter Brannen, "Earth Is Not in the Midst of a Sixth Mass Extinction," *The Atlantic,* June 13, 2017, https://www.theatlantic.com/science/archive/2017/06/the-ends-of-the-world/529545.

page 60: "If we could get the number of humans": Population Connection's "Carrying Capacity" at World Population History provides data regarding the numbers of humans over time. See https://worldpopulationhistory.org/carrying-capacity.

LONGING FOR WATER

page 63: My friend and former student Amina showed me a picture of her uncle in Kenya sharing his small pan of water with a thirsty warthog while other emaciated wild hogs looked on from behind.

6. LISTEN AND ACCEPT

page 65: "'My grandma told me about climate change'": While almost all dominant world cultures place some humans on the top of the importance pyramid and tend to think of the earth, nonhuman animals, plants, children, people of color, poor people, and women as resources, ecofeminism (also called ecowomanism) says that none of those are resources. Instead, ecofeminism acknowledges that we are all part of the network of life and must all be respected. Traditional feminism has tried to empower individual women to become as powerful as individual men; ecofeminism says that the whole is important and that there is no worthy reason for individual women to become as exploitative as some individual powerful men have been.

page 68: "Someone told me I had a pH of 5": Normal pH for humans is 7.4; normal ketone levels may be between .5 and 2.0, according to online sources.

8. FEEL THE GRIEF

page 86: "A study published": For information about the disproportionate effects of diabetes on populations of color, see Daniel Ruiz et al., "Disparities in Environmental Exposures to Endocrine-Disrupting Chemicals and Diabetes Risk in Vulnerable Populations," *Diabetes Care,* American Diabetes Association, January 1, 2018, https://care.diabetesjournals.org /content/41/1/193; Kelli Begay, Gina Gaviak, and LaShawn McIver, "A Call to Action: Eliminating Diabetes Disparities in Native Communities," *Clinical Diabetes,* American Diabetes Association, 2015, https://clinical .diabetesjournals.org/content/diaclin/33/4/206.full.pdf; and "Persistent Organic Pollutants: A Global Issue, a Global Response," Environmental Protection Agency, October 26, 2017, https://www.epa.gov/international -cooperation/persistent-organic-pollutants-global-issue-global-response.

page 90: "In 2018, more clarity arrived": For effects of air pollution on diabetes rates, see Benjamin Bowe et al., "The 2016 Global and National Burden of Diabetes Mellitus Attributable to $PM_{2.5}$ Air Pollution," *Lancet Planetary Health*, July 2018, https://doi.org/10.1016/S2542-5196(18)30140-2; and Purva Bhatter and Nerges Mistry, "Examining the Causal Link between and Air Pollution, Tuberculosis Type 2 Diabetes Mellitus," *Preprints*, 2018, https://doi.org/10.20944/preprints201801.0095.v1.

page 91: "In 1862, in the Minnesota River Valley": Little Crow's Dakota name is Taoyateduta. I feel humbled to be allowed to know and to speak the name by which he was known to his family. For historical information on the treatment of the Dakota people in Minnesota, see Minnesota Historical Society, "The U.S.–Dakota War of 1862," http://www.usdakotawar.org; and University of Minnesota College of Liberal Arts, "U.S.–Dakota War of 1862," https://cla.umn.edu/chgs/holocaust-genocide-education/resource-guides/us-dakota-war-1862.

9. CONNECT HUMBLY

page 96: "I was having trouble maintaining": A continuous glucose monitor, or CGM, includes a filament inserted about a quarter inch into the body (in my case, the wire is copper) that measures the sugar content of the interstitial fluid, the liquid bathing the cells.

page 99: "'We have to bring the racial justice'": For information on the weight of climate change and its impact first on less financially wealthy peoples, see "Goal 13: Take Urgent Action to Combat Climate Change and Its Impacts," United Nations, 2019, https://www.un.org/sustainabledevelopment/climate-change. For information about the impact of climate change on U.S. minority populations, see "Environmental and Climate Justice," NAACP, 2018, http://www.naacp.org/issues/environmental-justice.

10. ACCEPT BOTH

page 108: "Maybe we will learn to work": The Permaculture Research Institute Cold Climate (Minneapolis, 2019) gives a grounding in local restorative agriculture. See http://www.pricoldclimate.org.

page 111: "'Might you have calibrated'": Calibration, in relation to a continuous glucose monitor, is the act of informing the monitor of the actual

blood sugar readings so that it can correct its estimation of those readings against the readings it gets from the interstitial fluid.

page 118: "'Because the cannula I use'": Silhouette and Quick Set are both
Medtronic trade names for different insertion sets for a continuous
glucose monitor.

page 118: "But I had missed a decimal point": For a report on how pump fail-
ures are attributed to user error, see Holbrook Mohr and Mitch Weiss,
"AP Investigation: Insulin Pumps Have High Number of Injuries,"
Financial Post, November 27, 2018, https://business.financialpost
.com/pmn/business-pmn/ap-investigation-insulin-pumps-have-high
-number-of-injuries.

11. BEAR WITNESS

page 126: "In 2017, a twenty-six-year-old man": The parents of Alec Smith,
the young man who died because he did not have insurance to cover
insulin, led the fight in Minnesota for emergency insulin for those who
need it. At last, in April 2020, the Minnesota legislature passed the Alec
Smith Emergency Insulin Act. See https://www.minnpost.com/state
-government/2020/04/a-great-day-minnesota-legislature-finally-passes
-emergency-insulin-bill.

page 127: "I needed to understand how": Michael Bliss presents the history of
the events leading to the discovery of insulin in *The Discovery of Insulin*
(University of Toronto Press, 1982, 1996, 2017). See also Dan Hurley,
*Diabetes Rising: How a Rare Disease Became a Modern Pandemic, and
What to Do about It* (Kaplan Publishing, 2010).

page 128: "Diabetes was first considered": The labeling of types has become
even more complex. Some people are both type 1 and type 2.

page 129: "Hurley's fourth probable cause": Getting dirty in healthy soil and
around healthy animals is what Hurley suggests. This is not an argument
against protecting oneself and others from viruses like the coronavirus
by washing hands with soap and water, wearing protective masks and
clothing, and practicing social distancing while a pandemic is raging.

page 131: "at the upcoming Transition US National Gathering": Information
about the Transition US Gathering can be found at https://www
.transitiongathering.org. See also https://www.transitionus.org.

page 131: "Watching, he learned of permaculture": See http://www.pricold climate.org of the Permaculture Research Institute Cold Climate for information about Minnesota permaculture.

12. WALK WITH AND NOURISH OTHERS

page 136: "Adam Brown's book": See Adam Brown, *Bright Spots and Landmines: The Diabetes Guide I Wish Someone Had Handed Me* (diaTribe Foundation, 2017).

page 138: "Just before insulin was developed": Thea Cooper and Arthur Ainsberg give a solidly researched story about the development of insulin and the first children to receive it in *Breakthrough: Elizabeth Hughes, the Discovery of Insulin, and the Making of a Medical Miracle* (St. Martin's Griffin, 2011).

page 138: "On the days when she ate at all": Lewis Webb Hill and Rena Sarah Eckman, *The Allen (Starvation) Treatment of Diabetes, with a Series of Graduated Diets* (Leonard, 1929) has been reprinted as an essential historical document. It provides information about how people in the past lived with diabetes.

page 139: "Soil is alive": Further information about Winona LaDuke and Ojibwe ethics can be found at Honor the Earth, http://www.honorearth.org/about.

page 140: "Learn the names of plants, or give them names yourself": Robin Wall Kimmerer, author of *Braiding Sweetgrass: Indigenous Wisdom, Scientific Knowledge, and the Teachings of Plants* (Milkweed, 2013), suggests the use of a new singular pronoun, *ki*, instead of "it," to refer to the other beings who share our world. The plural form, *kin*, would clearly indicate our connection with these other beings. See https://vimeo.com/488276804?fbclid=IwAR2gg6_AGurNVoEaG-mbuc9LxS VoCKWLviibjDa_FUHNPj4uM7dTgvFyGgQ.

13. WATER, PLANT, AND MAKE SOIL

page 141: "Group after group of Somali students": Nobel Peace Prize winner Wangari Maathai inspired and led the Green Belt Movement and wrote *Unbowed: A Memoir* (Anchor, 2006), *The Green Belt Movement: Sharing the Approach and the Experience* (Lantern, 2003), and *The Challenge for Africa* (Anchor, 2009). Students read *Unbowed* in my class.

page 141: "With aid from wise teachers": As a start to reading Dakota wisdom, I suggest Joseph M. Marshall's *The Lakota Way: Stories and Lessons for Living; Native American Wisdom on Ethics and Character* (Penguin, 2002). For written Ojibwe teachings, I suggest Mary Siisip Geniusz, *Plants Have So Much to Give Us, All We Have to Do Is Ask: Anishinaabe Botanical Teachings* (University of Minnesota Press, 2015), and Linda LeGarde Grover, *Onigamiising: Seasons of an Ojibwe Year* (University of Minnesota Press, 2017).

page 144: "Over the months, Julie reported back": You can learn more about Julie Ristau and Najwa Bukari's work on the Mainstreet Project at https://mainstreetproject.org. For further information about permaculture, see https://permacultureprinciples.com. The term "permaculture" is most correctly applied only to Native American agricultural practices, but at the time I was writing it was also used for non-Native practices that, at the time of this publication, are more commonly called restorative agriculture.

page 146: "Contact with soil microbes": Bonnie L. Grant's "Antidepressant Microbes in Soil: How Dirt Makes You Happy" from *Gardening Know How* ("Best Plants: Tips for the Soil and Garden") interprets research about depression-fighting microbes found in soil. https://www.gardeningknowhow.com/garden-how-to/soil-fertilizers/antidepressant-microbes-soil.htm.

COMING HOME

page 147: "You may walk the length of a river": Sharon Day, Ojibwe elder, invites readers to Nibi Water Walks at http://www.nibiwalk.org and then to join her and others in a walk to honor water.

14. FOG

page 149: "In 2018, I attended a talk": For a recording of the lecture by Kenny Blumenfeld, see https://www.swac.umn.edu/spring-2018 ("Managing

Minnesota's Changing Climatology and the Case for Myopia," University of Minnesota, Department of Soil, Water, and Climate, Spring 2018 Seminar Series, January 24, 2018).

page 150: "Blumenfeld laid out what we do know": The lowest low seems, to me, alarmingly higher than Blumenfeld predicted. In January 2020 at Birch Lake, St. Louis County, the lowest low was −25.

page 156: "In the material handed out at the conference": In *Climate Change Indicators in the United States, 2016* (United States Environmental Protection Agency, 2016), Christopher M. Barker et al. provide indicators of climate change effects in the United States and explain connections between climate change and health.

page 159: "Banting and John Macleod": Michael Bliss presents the history of the events leading to the discovery of insulin in *The Discovery of Insulin*, 25th anniversary ed. (University of Toronto Press, 2000).

15. MIRACLES, MYSTERY, AND DREAMS

page 163: "It was the middle of the night": For information about the men who first brought insulin to people with diabetes, see Bliss, *The Discovery of Insulin.*

16. WHEN THE TIME COMES

page 168: "Other students described climate devastation": For a recording of the session, see https://www.youtube.com/watch?v=CRpM1C7vDBU&list=PLCbcUfyW-bUuqOTsmC2cQdSPEJyjRMrX_&index=7.

page 169: "I researched other ways for diabetics": Lewis Webb Hill and Rena Sarah Eckman's *The Allen (Starvation) Treatment of Diabetes, with a Series of Graduated Diets* (Leonard, 1929) has been reprinted as an essential historical document. It provides information about how some people survived diabetes before insulin.

page 170: "Yet, many are searching for a way": For further information about permaculture, see https://permacultureprinciples.com; for information about the attempt to bring back the Siberian grasslands, see Ross Andersen, "Welcome to Pleistocene Park," *The Atlantic* (April 2017), https://www.theatlantic.com/magazine/archive/2017/04/pleistocene-park/517779.

For information about vertical ocean farming, see the TED Talk by Bren Smith, "Vertical Ocean Farming: The Least Deadliest Catch," https://ideas.ted.com/vertical-ocean-farms-that-can-feed-us-and-help -our-seas.

17. RETURN

page 177: "Pinecones open only during fire": I was wrong to apply this to white pinecones. Since hearing the old pine speak, I've paid closer attention. Young white pines line many forest roads where no fire has passed.

18. MAY YOUR WATERSHED LIVE—AND YOU WITH IT

page 183: Refugee students have reported that their grandparents or parents told them to leave their homelands because the water was gone. Becky Gawboy said to me, "Mother Earth is rebalancing. Trust her."

CODA

page 187: Further information about Ojibwe ethics and Winona LaDuke's work can be found at Honor the Earth, http://www.honorearth.org/about. LaDuke and other Indigenous people have said in my hearing that the original ethical principles were to be passed from living tongues to living ears and stored in living brains so that they could change as conditions in the world and in people shifted. Making the words permanent by engraving them on paper from trees that have been killed has been seen as wrong. However, the guideline against writing the principles was itself altered once too few living brains and tongues and ears remained to carry the memory. The basic wisdom stands: living things continually change, and ethical principles should shift to suit them. Remember to alter these principles as wisdom and conditions around you demand.

Born into a community of storytellers in the northern watersheds of Minnesota, **Ranae Lenor Hanson** has been an educator for forty-five years. She often collaborates with Minnesota 350, Transition US, and other organizations to develop effective responses to the trauma of our changing climate. In the 1980s she worked in administration for several residential mental health treatment centers. She holds a PhD in education and recently retired from teaching after thirty-one years at Minneapolis College. She lives in St. Paul.